Work-Related Learning and the Social Sciences

Work-Related Learning and the Social Sciences provides a clear and accessible introduction to the theory and practice of work. Written in a student-friendly style, it makes use of the following:

- *Theoretical perspectives*: The theoretical foundations of identity, power, community, citizenship, experiential learning and a range of employability skills provide frameworks for the chapters.
- *Key issues*: The book addresses such issues as: How are people socialised at work? Why does conflict occur at work? What types of control are exerted at work? What can we learn about our communities from the work we do? How can we develop our employability skills?
- *Sector examples*: Extensive use is made of examples of the working practices of teachers, social workers, police officers, civil servants and third sector workers, as well as from people engaged in low-skilled work.
- *The student voice*: The student voice draws upon the relationship between his or her own experiences of work and the key issues covered in the book.

Written as an introductory text for students studying the social sciences, it deals with the ways in which students can appreciate the sociology and politics of work and develop an understanding of their own skills and employability. This book is particularly relevant to students studying work-related learning as part of their social science degrees and to those who wish to enhance their employability and prospects in graduate-level employment.

Gary Taylor is principal lecturer in the Department of Psychology, Sociology and Politics at Sheffield Hallam University. He has written a number of books on social and political theory, social policy and on the media.

Liam Mellor currently works at Certara, a private sector consultancy provider specialising in drug discovery and development software. He has degrees from both Sheffield Hallam University (sociology) and Sheffield University (political communication) and has worked on a range of publications.

Richard McCarter is senior lecturer in the Faculty of Development and Society at Sheffield Hallam University, teaching in the Department of Education and also the Department of Psychology, Sociology and Politics. His interest is technology enhanced learning and e-portfolios, but he also has a background in educational television.

Work-Related Learning and the Social Sciences

Gary Taylor, Liam Mellor and Richard McCarter

Routledge
Taylor & Francis Group

LONDON AND NEW YORK

First published 2016
by Routledge
2 Park Square, Milton Park, Abingdon, Oxon OX14 4RN

and by Routledge
711 Third Avenue, New York, NY 10017

Routledge is an imprint of the Taylor & Francis Group, an informa business

British Library Cataloguing-in-Publication Data
A catalogue record for this book is available from the British Library

Library of Congress Cataloging-in-Publication Data
Taylor, Gary
  Work-related learning and the social sciences / by Gary Taylor, Liam
Mellor and Richard McCarter.
       pages cm
  1. Vocational guidance.   2. Employee motivation.   3. Job skills.
4. Career development.   5. Experiential learning.   6. Organizational
learning.   7. Industrial sociology.   I. Mellor, Liam.   II. McCarter,
Richard.   III. Title.
   HF5381.T2357 2015
   300.71—dc23
   2015016522

ISBN: 978-1-138-80433-3 (hbk)
ISBN: 978-1-138-80434-0 (pbk)
ISBN: 978-1-315-75307-2 (ebk)

Typeset in Bembo
by Apex CoVantage
Printed and bound in Great Britain by Ashford Colour Press Ltd, Gosport, Hampshire

Contents

Acknowledgements

We would like to thank a number of people for their help and encouragement while we were writing this book. Thanks to the Higher Education Academy for the generous teaching development grant that allowed us some time to work on particular sections. We have also benefitted greatly from our conversations with colleagues at Sheffield Hallam University, who continue to use their creative talents to look for ways to integrate employability into the curriculum. Our friends and colleagues Malcolm Todd, Luke Desforges, Emma Heron, Joy Drever and Mike McManus have been very supportive. Our thanks also go to Dave Laughton, Bridget Winwood, Jeff Waldock, Charmaine Myers, Pat Quinn and Paul Helm. Alan Wigfield helped to identify some interesting sources on low-skilled work, and we benefitted greatly from his thoughtful contributions in numerous conversations. We also thank our students for granting us permission to recount some of their stories. Gerhard Boomgaarden, Catherine Gray and Alyson Claffey at Routledge have all been generous with their support and guidance throughout the process of writing the book. We would also like to thank our three anonymous reviewers for their comments on the original proposal and for suggesting ways to improve the manuscript. Thanks, finally, to our partners and families who have endured our absence and spurred us on. Karen in particular has been wonderful in reading the chapters, asking questions and providing comments.

chapter 1

Introduction

Work-related learning is becoming an increasingly important feature of studying at degree level. Relatively few university students now participate in higher education with little or no regard for future employment. The costs of higher education are such that many students need some paid employment to help finance their studies and will often be motivated in part by the belief that a degree will help them to secure some interesting and well-paid work in the future. A degree in itself, however, is no longer enough to gain access to graduate-level work. Graduates often find that they have to prove not only that they have the qualifications necessary for graduate-level work but that they also have the skills, attributes and awareness necessary to secure employment at that level. Work-related learning can help students to develop their understanding of the world of work and to recognise their own abilities. This development can take place through internships, working on voluntary sector projects or through learning to reflect upon their current part-time employment. Regardless of where students gain their experiences of work, it is important that they learn from these experiences and start to develop awareness of their skills, interests and capabilities. For students in the social sciences, this can sometimes be challenging. Although students studying such subjects as Sociology, Politics, Psychology and Criminology are not generally training for a particular career, such degrees are packed with transferable skills and, given the opportunity to explore these, students studying the social sciences can leave university with plenty to offer a wide range of employers. This book seeks to illustrate to students studying the social sciences the benefits of studying work, of reflecting upon their own abilities and of enhancing their own employability.

Work

Work plays an important part in influencing the way people see themselves and associate with others. It influences the way people view their own identity and how they come to recognise their own potential. Svendsen (2008) notes that through participating in work, workers learn '. . . about our own abilities, our relations to others, and our role in the social fabric' (Svendsen, 2008, p. 10). Zygmunt Bauman's challenging treatise on *Liquid Modernity* gives work a defining role in solidifying the social world and it is seen as part of the ' . . . modern ambition to subdue, harness and colonize the future in order to replace chaos with order and contingency with a predictable (and so controllable) sequence of events' (Bauman, 2000, p. 137). It would be wrong, however, to believe that the relationship between work and social values is in some way automatic or predetermined. People are generally free to determine the value they place upon work and to consider how best to pursue employment-related goals. These goals could include self-fulfilment in work, vocational service as well as more instrumental attitudes towards employment.

The spiritual significance of work

Running through the current volume is the assertion that the true value of work lies beyond what it can provide financially. Work can be a means to an end in the sense of providing an income necessary to pursue leisure activities or live a certain lifestyle, but that does not mean workers are untouched at the core by the work they do. Those who are interested in these broader spiritual questions may well find comfort in the romantic assertion that work allows people to access knowledge of themselves and ways to develop their own characters. This is not about discovering an essential self that lies buried within, but about people taking charge of their own development and forging new possibilities for themselves. According to this line of thought, it is through work that people engage in the process of 'self-fashioning' and come to understand their 'authentic self' (Svendsen, 2008, pp. 25–27). Even if we are not willing to go this far, perhaps because we want to trace our fundamental essence to things other than work or deny that we have a fundamental essence to trace, the romantic paradigm provides a way to recognise the fluid nature of work and to see how work can enhance self-development. This development is by no means always beneficial. Although illusions about work can (and perhaps should) be shattered, they are invariably replaced by other theoretical perspectives on work.

Those who work will invariably have opinions about the work they do. This book aims in part to trace some ways to structure these opinions and make sense of work by gaining an appreciation of the multitude of ways it can influence how people view themselves and their place in society.

The political significance of work

When discussing how individuals behave in the workplace and the skills they can cultivate through their own efforts, there is relatively little need to place individuals in a broad social context and to consider how they can have a beneficial impact upon society. As soon as we locate the individual in the community and reveal that individuals have a key role in brokering trust, then the political significance of the individual becomes more apparent. A reasonably radical agenda can be developed by factoring into our analysis some of the ways that people are linked into the global network. According to Beck (2000), the main social problems stemming from globalisation, environmental destruction and the changing pattern of employment cannot be solved by citizens working in small geographical areas, but they rely rather more upon the development of a broader sense of belonging. As a job for life or indeed a single career is in decline for many people, it might be necessary to embrace uncertainty and develop the ability to perform a variety of tasks and to work in a more flexible manner (Beck, 2000). As the security once afforded to workers is in decline, it could well be that many people will experience the need to engage with the community and to promote their skills and abilities as their working lives are transformed.

Work-related learning

Work-related learning provides an opportunity to study work and to consider its broader impact upon workers. According to Raelin (2008), learning through work can be viewed '. . . as a natural process tied to the human instinct to grow. In this sense, it is very much a part of our being (Raelin, 2008, p. 5). Gray, Cundell, Hay and O'Neil (2004) claim that for most people learning takes place throughout their lives. This can occur via everyday experiences, including those within the workplace. They argue that learning through work is primarily informal and takes place when workers reflect upon their experiences. Billett (2008) claims that work-related learning involves learning through experience, making decisions and making mistakes as well as learning the values tied to this learning environment. According to Tomlinson (2013), work-related learning takes place both on a formal and informal level. Formal work-related learning can be delivered in a predetermined way and for a specific purpose. Informal learning will also take place as workers adapt to the working environment and develop influential relationships with their colleagues. This informal learning takes place as a result of participating in the work process and is '. . . based on their experiences in social environments and the interactions this inevitably entails' (Tomlinson, 2013, p.127). This form of learning can be particularly powerful and tends to be valued by many employers, who '. . . often view experiential learning opportunities as ultimately producing more competent entry-level professionals' (Alderman and Milne, 2005, p. 3). Although a fairly instrumental approach to work-related learning might concentrate upon the accumulation of skills valued by employers, this should not obscure the ways in which learning through work can complement and enrich other forms of learning.

Learning does not need to be abstract to be of value. Indeed, learning anchored in reflections on work can incorporate, challenge and supplement what can be gained from studying social and political theory. Fuller and Unwin (2005) reject the view that learning that takes place in structured educational settings is superior to the dynamic learning that takes place in the work environment. This learning can be informal as well as deliberate and can take place because workers learn how to participate with others and determine how to learn what they need to know. It is clear, however, that there will always be limits placed upon learning within the workplace. Billet (2004) claims that the ability to learn through work rest upon the relationship between individual participants and the opportunities provided by the workplace. Individuals may choose to participate in a variety of learning opportunities but these will always be limited by the value placed upon particular forms of learning by the employers. Because of this, learning within the workplace is carried out within the context of power relations. Although individuals might wish to develop particular skills, they will find it difficult to do so without the support of their employers. He claims, indeed, that conflict is unavoidable as '. . . power and personal politics are played out, and there will always be tensions between the goals of the enterprise and the individual' (Billett, 2004, p. 122).

Active learning

The lessons learnt through work are not easily summarised by another but require workers to think their way through their experiences and be engaged as active learners. Active learning involves learners behaving as active participants in the learning process rather than as passive recipients of transmitted knowledge. This participation requires the learner to reflect, analyse, synthesise and evaluate (McManus and Taylor, 2009). Boud (2001) urges work-based learners to become active participants in the learning process and '. . . confident that one's learning needs can be met, developing an identity as an active learner and taking a proactive stance towards the challenges that confront one in the workplace' (Boud, 2001, p. 49). This may require learners to rethink what learning involves and reconsider their role within the learning process. Successful work-related learning programmes can contribute to the development of lifelong learning by helping learners to appreciate their existing achievements, recognise their knowledge, plan for future learning and critically reflect on understanding and document achievements (Boud, 2001). It has been noted that successful work-related learning schemes can enhance a person's self-confidence, self-efficacy and belief in their own power to learn and perform (Stephenson, 2001). Work-related learning can encourage people to take greater control over their lives and perhaps even design their own work in line with their abilities, values and aspirations. This is not merely about careers, but about how work fits into everything else people do.

The importance of reflection

So how do people learn through work? Part of this relies upon learning how to reflect, which involves considering aspects of '. . . learning, learning though problem-solving and learning about learning itself' (Gray, Cundell, Hay and O'Neil, 2004, p. 4). In comparison to traditional academic learning, work-related learning is not concerned simply with acquiring knowledge and skills. It has far more to do with nourishing the ability to reflect upon experiences. This reflection can take place individually and collectively. The latter can be particularly useful in helping to create and reinforce shared values and a vibrant community of practice (Raelin, 2008). We should remember that for the majority of people, work takes place within a collective or social setting and relies upon the individual engaging to some extent with other people. Gray et al. (2004) note that you '. . . construct your own experience in the context of a particular setting and range of cultural values that you, and others, hold. Your environment can both inhibit and encourage you to learn from the experiences you meet' (Gray et al., 2004, p. 116). It is important to note that not all jobs are conducive with constructive and shared reflection. Indeed, individuals can sometimes only survive some forms of work by learning how to 'switch off' and to forget about work as rapidly as possible. This does not mean there is no room for reflection. The desire to move away from what they do and try other things is a powerful incentive, and the prospect of changing jobs or careers can be enhanced by the ability to reflect upon the range of skills that they could offer another employer.

Reflection and the input of others

The reflective process does not need to be solitary or take place in isolation of the input of others. The advice picked up from colleagues can sometimes be extremely useful in helping to direct the attention of workers towards potential areas for development. According to Raelin (2008), it is often the case that people fail to consider the effects of their actions upon others and that this lack of awareness can prevent them from taking on board useful advice. However, shared experiences can help to inform, influence and possibly change behaviour and it is '. . . often only through the support of and feedback from others that we can become receptive to alternative ways of reasoning and behaving . . . such an awareness is extremely difficult to awaken without the involvement of peers who can detect the use of untested assumptions and raw biases' (Raelin, 2008, pp. 127–128). Although the input and advice of others can be useful, it is the ability to reflect that allows people '. . . to search for truths even if they are unpleasant to us, to take personal casual responsibility for problems, and to allow us to accept some pain in order to learn how to become a better societal participant' (Raelin, 2008, p. 136). Developing the ability to reflect does not entail aimlessly pondering possibilities but involves people scrutinising their own attitudes, actions and experiences and seeing these as influencing how they develop in the future. Learning how to reflect in the workplace might not save workers from making mistakes, but it should enable them to limit making the same mistakes continuously. It can also provide people with a useful way to gauge what they do in terms of its impact on themselves and on others and to take more control over how they approach their work and plan their careers.

It is clear that the workplace can be an important centre for learning. For Raelin (2008), work-related learning offers an opportunity to utilise the workplace as a means of enhancing a person's learning experience rather than simply focusing on the classroom as the primary environment for learning. Fuller, Munro and Rainbird (2004b) argue that it is important to recognise that work-related learning does not take place in a politically neutral environment and that '. . . opportunities and barriers are structured and unevenly distributed across organisations and different groups' (Fuller et al., 2004b, p. 3). The ability of individuals to assume complete responsibility for their own learning is limited because of deeply ingrained inequalities in power between employers and employees (Fuller et al., 2004a). Despite these limitations, work-related learning allows people to explore connections between academic and experiential learning, theory and practice and encourages them to search for synergies between academic knowledge and the experiences accumulated through work. We should note, moreover, that allowing individuals to learn from their experiences of work might help to bring some balance to their lives. By separating work from the rest of life and turning working into nothing more than a means to an end, work can be reduced to a force that depletes the energy of the individual. Whilst accepting that there is some truth to this, being open to learning through work could help the individual to develop new interests and to stretch his or her own capabilities.

The structure of the book

The current volume has two main aims. The first is to provide a theoretical framework to explore the nature of work and how it can impact upon the individual and society. This is referred to as *learning about work*. The second aim is to provide students with some ways to make the most of their experiences of work and to prepare for their careers after graduation. The term *learning through work* is used to capture these dimensions of the book. It should be evident, however, that these two approaches to work are related. What can be learnt *about* work can also help an individual learn *through* work. For example, somebody who studies patterns of authority and power in the teaching profession could be attracted to or put off pursuing a career in this area because of what they discover academically. The same could be said about the impact of *learning through work*. The way people reflect upon their experiences of work can in turn encourage them to take more interest in *learning about work* in that particular sector. Whilst remaining mindful of the possible connections between these two main aims, the book will be divided into two sections and will deal with *learning about work* and *learning through work* respectively.

Part One: Learning about work: Theoretical frameworks

The first part of the book is concerned primarily with *learning about work* through a series of theoretical frameworks. These frameworks look at the impact of work upon individual identity, understanding of power relations and the way people view their own place in the community. These issues have been selected because they should be reasonably familiar to students in the social sciences. Identity, power and community will be treated as frameworks necessary to understand the broader social and political significance of work. We will ask how people learn about work, how they can find fulfilment in their work and how they can locate themselves in their communities through the work they do. How does work mould individual identities? Why can work be an alienating process? What mechanisms are used to control people at work? Why does conflict occur at work and how do workers respond? What can be done to enhance social capital? What responsibilities do people have as citizens and how does work help them to understand these? When studying work, we will be attempting to capture a variety of experiences and address a range of important social and political issues.

Part Two: Learning through work: Skills development

Part two of the book concentrates on outlining some processes involved in experiential learning and looks at how people can take more control over their own working lives through being aware of their own personal development, taking stock of the skills they have and those they need to develop and how they can increase their understanding of their own employability. This section of the book begins by identifying some of the distinctive features of experiential learning. We will see how experiences of work can be recorded, analysed and made use of in personal and professional development. We will then move on to take a look at some important work-related skills, including leadership, teamwork, communication, problem solving, decision making and creativity. We conclude this section of the book by addressing the relationship between skills and employability. Although it is possible to develop work-related skills in an incremental and quite purposeful way, employability relies upon workers being aware of what they have to offer potential employers and in making connections between their various abilities and attributes. This form of learning is cast as *learning through work* as each person becomes the subject of his or her own study.

The structure of the chapters

Each chapter will address the connections between a variety of concepts. In part one of the book, theoretical frameworks will be constructed by making use of important social theorists including Bauman, Beck, Marx, Foucault and Putnam. It is not our intention to provide a comprehensive examination of these theorists and their contribution to social and political thought but to investigate how their ideas can be used to discuss the nature and significance of work. In the second part of the book, the material on learning through work is considered through a range of key employability skills. By examining some of the links between these theoretical frameworks and employability skills, we will attempt to make sense of some of the complexities of work and show how work touches people in a multitude of ways and contributes towards their appreciation of the relationship between their activities and their sense of belonging.

The book will also make use of examples from a variety of sectors of employment. Whilst this volume is by no means a history of work, examples will be drawn to illuminate the frameworks and skills outlined earlier from low-skilled work and from selected professions. The material on low-skilled work includes examples from employment in such sectors as catering, call centres and hotels. It could be that such examples resonate particularly well with students who find themselves working their way through university by taking on employment in these areas. Examples are also used from social work, teaching, police and the third sector of voluntary groups and charities. These examples have been included because these professions tend to be attractive to graduates in the social sciences.

Having introduced theoretical frameworks, explored key skills and included examples from different sectors of employment, each chapter will also take a closer look at key debates. This will provide us with an opportunity to drill down into an issue and reveal some of the complexities of work. In part one of the book, these debates will include coverage of emotional labour, the working environment, zero-hours contracts, change management and social responsibility. Part two of the book explores key employability skills and considers the processes by which people learn through work and prepare themselves for graduate-level work.

Some use will also be made of students' reflections on their own experience of work. In many cases, they capture their struggles to combine full-time education and part-time employment. Although students are often employed in low-skilled occupations, it is possible to gain some insight into how they draw a connection between their two worlds of employment and study and how they can make sense of their experiences through their reflections. We will also see how students attempt to gain an understanding of their skills in preparation for their possible transition into the professions. It is hoped that these examples will help to reveal to a student audience the relevance of some of the more theoretical material contained herein.

Conclusion

So the journey begins. We identify at the outset that work has an important impact upon the way people see themselves and relate to others and suggest what can be learnt through reflecting upon the work process. This book is not about what we should learn from work. Although it recognises that people will have different experiences of work and will draw different lessons from their work, it is suggested that work permeates individual and social identities and that it is possible to deconstruct work and work-related skills. Work-related learning involves learning through, about and for work. It provides an opportunity to see work within a broader social and political context and to explore ways to approach professional development. Although it is hoped that this approach to work-related learning will help students in the social sciences to develop their own career paths, it is important that we do not lose sight of the individual, social and political significance of work. It sees work and the work process as a legitimate source of concern for social scientists and provides a series of ways to explore the connections between people.

References

Alderman, B. and Milne, P. (2005) *A Model for Work-Based Learning*, The Scarecrow Press: Maryland.

Bauman, Z. (2000) *Liquid Modernity*, Polity: Cambridge.

Beck, U. (2000) *The Brave New World of Work*, Polity Press: Cambridge.

Billett, S. (2004) 'Learning through work: Workplace participatory practices'. In Rainbird, H., Fuller, A. and Munro, A. (eds) (2004) *Workplace Learning in Context*, Routledge: London, pp. 109–125.

Billett, S. (2008) 'Emerging perspectives on workplace learning'. In Billett, S., Harteis, C. and Etelapelto, A. (eds) (2008) *Emerging Perspectives of Workplace Learning*, Sense Publishers: Rotterdam, pp. 1–16.

Boud, D. (2001) 'Creating a work-based curriculum'. In D. Boud and N. Solomon (eds) (2001) *Work-Based Learning: A New Higher Education?* The Society for Research into Higher Education and Open University Press: Berkshire, pp. 44–58.

Fuller, A., Munro, A. and Rainbird, H. (2004a) 'Conclusion'. In Rainbird, H., Fuller, A. and Munro, A. (eds) (2004) *Workplace Learning in Context*, Routledge: London, pp. 299–306.

Fuller, A., Munro, A. and Rainbird, H. (2004b) 'Introduction and overview'. In Rainbird, H., Fuller, A. and Munro, A. (eds) (2004) *Workplace Learning in Context*, Routledge: London, pp. 1–18.

Fuller, A. and Unwin, A. (2005) 'Older and wiser?: Workplace learning from the perspective of experienced workers', *International Journal of Lifelong Education*, Volume 24, Issue 1, pp. 21–39.

Gray, D., Cundell, S., Hay, D. and O'Neil, J. (2004) *Learning Through the Workplace: A Guide to Work-Based Learning*, Nelson Thornes Ltd: Cheltenham.

McManus, M. and Taylor, G. (2009) 'Introduction'. In M. McManus and G. Taylor (eds) *Active Learning and Active Citizenship: Theoretical Contexts*, Higher Education Academy: Birmingham, pp. 9–29.

Raelin, J.A. (2008) *Work-Based Learning: Bridging Knowledge and Action in the Workplace*, Jossey-Bass: San Francisco.

Stephenson, J. (2001) 'Ensuring a holistic approach to work-based learning: The capability envelope'. In D. Boud and N. Solomon (eds) (2001) *Work-Based Learning: A New Higher Education?* The Society for Research into Higher Education and Open University Press: Berkshire, pp. 86–102.

Svendsen, L. (2008) *Work*, Acumen: Durham.

Tomlinson, M. (2013) *Education, Work and Identity*, Bloomsbury: London.

Learning about work

Theoretical frameworks

chapter 2

Identity, Socialisation and Emotional Labour

In constructing frameworks to use to examine the impact of work on the individual and society, it makes sense to begin with the individual and try to identify the impact of work upon individual identity. When people choose a job or profession, they say something about themselves, even if this is temporary and is later subject to radical change. When taking on a job or career, people tend to become defined by what they do. But the impact of work upon identity is by no means simple, mainly because work is far from a stable badge of status. The experience people have of work will be important in determining whether they see work as a positive force in the enrichment of their lives or as a drain on their sense of who they are. This will change as they enter a new job, settle into a new routine and as they develop their careers. People will be influenced by the tasks they are expected to perform, the relationships they have with colleagues and the values of the organisation for which they work. This chapter will focus upon the impact of work on identity, the ways people are socialised in work and the struggle people have with their emotions at work. Rather than seeing work as a unifying force or as something that gives permanent meaning to the lives of people, we will see that there is an expectation that people will change and adapt in the work they do and that these changes can sometimes be disruptive to the individual.

Identity and work

Identity is both personal and social. It is concerned with an 'internal sense of self' and the allocation of positions in society. The identities people have are by no means stable and unchanging. They are influenced through social interactions and the way people define themselves will fluctuate with changes in culture. Although it might be tempting to believe that identities are fixed and stable, it could be argued that identities are in a state of flux and that it is important to deconstruct identities rather than attempt to define them (Taylor and Spencer, 2004). Although a distinction can be made between personal identity and social identity, these two forms of identity are definitely linked. Sense of self could be viewed as a purely individual construction spurred on by some existentialist need, but it should be evident that it is also influenced by the judgements made by other people and that these judgements will often be influenced by a person's social makeup. In addition to providing a way for an individual to understand him or herself, identity can also be viewed as the framework of values that can be used when determining how to act in particular situations. Identity is not passive or something that is possessed in isolation but is something that spurs people to interact with the social world in particular ways (Tomlinson, 2013). The autonomy of people to construct their own identities according to their interests is limited by the resources at their disposal and by their place in social networks. Their identity will evolve as they navigate and negotiate their way through social life. When we talk about identity, we need to recognise its dynamic nature and appreciate that identities are influenced constantly by a range of individual and social factors, including the work people do.

The significance of work

The extent to which work is significant for individual identity is open to debate. Its importance has been acknowledged by scholars, even if this importance is contextualised in the light of the changing nature of work and the increasing importance of leisure. Beck (2000), for example, claims that work attributes workers with truly human characteristics in the sense it has '. . . become part of the self understanding of people who form, revalue and naturalise their own identity and personality only in and through work' (Beck, 2000, p. 13). Work is viewed by de Botton (2009) as being far more important than money as a key determinant of identity. Indeed, work can be seen as central to the meaning people attribute to their lives since '. . . the route to a meaningful existence must invariably pass through the gate of remunerative employment' (de Botton, 2009, p.106). There are numerous benefits to being in employment and these go far beyond its financial rewards. Coats and Max (2005) point out that friendships and emotional bonds are established at work and that work can also improve individual well-being by helping to reduce stress, obesity and heart disease. Holding down a job allows many people to pursue their aspirations and it can help keep people motivated and alert (see Dight, 2007). Work can, in a multitude of ways, enhance a person's sense of self. It is something that can give meaning to their lives and provide the kind of stimulus it is difficult to find in any other way. Apart from anything else, the friendships and relationships people develop at work can be enriching and significant.

The value placed upon the importance of work will certainly differ between individuals. Not everybody will regard their work as a foundation for their sense of self. People will differ quite considerably in the way they view work. Svendsen (2008) distinguishes between internal and external goods. Internal goods include fulfilment and happiness at work. External goods relate more often than not to financial rewards. In his view, it is important for people to choose jobs that are compatible with their own value system. This involves determining the relative importance of the internal and external benefits deriving from work and attempting to secure a suitable balance between these (see Svendsen, 2008). It would appear that for those who concern themselves primarily with the external goods generated through work, the intrinsic value of work is superseded by the belief that work is a means to an end. Regardless of economic position, many people attempt to enhance their sense of well-being and express their identity through their ownership of material goods and use these to define themselves and make distinctions between their own lives and the lives of others (see Macintosh and Mooney, 2000). It is evident that people do not enter a work setting free from their own expectations of work and from their own particular value systems. What people make of work will often depend upon how they choose to set priorities in their lives and the value they place upon creativity, autonomy and social responsibility, as well as the need to satisfy their own particular material wants and desires. What individuals gain from work is thus dependent upon the criteria they use to attribute meaning and significance to their activities. It is important to be mindful of this subjective element, as it can help people to understand the roots of their own attitudes towards work and provide them with a way to appreciate the priorities and motivations of their colleagues.

Bauman on flexible labour, identity and pleasure

The ideas of Zygmunt Bauman can alert us to the changing nature of work and the importance of recognising the place and limitations of work in the construction of identity. Bauman (1998) claims that workers are discouraged from viewing their work as permanent and stable and from developing any mature narrative about the rights and responsibilities tied to their particular job. In his view, labour must '... unlearn its hard-trained dedication to work and its hard-won emotional attachment to the workplace. . .' (Bauman, 1998, p. 112). The need to be flexible in the labour market discourages people from showing commitment to a particular job or career. This makes perfect sense for '... embracing one's work as a vocation carries enormous risks and is a recipe for psychological and emotional disaster' (Bauman, 2005, p. 35). Bauman (2000) argues that although work once defined identities, it has lost its central determining role and '. . . can no longer offer the secure axis around which to wrap and fix self-definitions, identities and life-projects' (Bauman, 2000, p. 139). If people can no longer expect to remain in the same job for life, then any impact of a particular job upon personal identity is likely to be transitory. Rather than attempting to define themselves by using a single job or occupation, many people will be forced to reinvent themselves as workers, refresh their skills and revise their priorities.

The transitory nature of each particular identity at work stems not only from instabilities within the labour market and the demand for workers in particular sectors but also from the way many people construct their careers in the hope of maximising pleasure at work and to satisfy their changing expectations of work. Bauman (2005) notes that social status is increasingly influenced by what people consume and that this can be seen partly as a result of a steady but significant decline in traditional career paths. Whereas people once made choices about the career they wished to pursue and proceeded in incremental steps to develop the expertise and status attributed to that career, this is no longer necessarily the case. Individuals are now expected to enter a variety of jobs and even careers rather than follow a lifetime vocation in one particular area. This is not to say that work no longer has an impact upon personal identity. Rather than define who they are for all time, people are expected to adopt the identities necessary to function in particular roles. Although work might be less secure, more flexible and more chaotic, work will still have an impact upon personal identity. With each change in role, workers abandon particular identities and take on new identities (see box 2a for an illustration of how this can happen). These identities, moreover, can be viewed in the same way as consumer goods. They can be possessed by individuals, enjoyed for some time and jettisoned when they are no longer necessary or fulfilling.

When we talk about flexible labour, we need to avoid seeing all workers as passive victims of the fickle economic cycle and acknowledge that many workers will change occupations because they are searching for something that eludes them in their current employment. Bauman (2000) believes that people expect to be amused or entertained by the work they do and that work has somehow attained aesthetic significance. Rather than seeing work as something that builds character and allows people to contribute towards the general good, people have become preoccupied with the way work makes them feel. Whereas career choices used to say a lot about an individual and provide a person with a means of self-expression and even moral development, Bauman argues that work is now judged primarily on aesthetic terms and '. . . by its capacity to generate pleasurable experience' (Bauman, 2005, p. 33). People will no doubt value interesting, fulfilling and varied work, especially in a society that emphasises the importance of the pleasure to be gained from consumption. Using Bauman's insights into the changing nature of work and its importance for individual identity, it is possible to see that workers can play a proactive role in choosing the work they do. Workers are increasingly willing to change occupations, start to work with a new group of colleagues and find that the identity they created for themselves in their previous occupation is no longer satisfactory or useful in the jobs they move on to.

Work cultures

Work cultures refer to the values developed at particular places of work that provide a framework and set of expectations for workers. These cultures can be particularly important in encouraging workers to forge bonds with their colleagues and to develop a shared ethos at work. Each work setting will have its own culture. Sometimes this is created by management and established around a set of core values. When entering employment, it makes sense to try to understand the prevailing culture at work. This will allow the worker to judge the extent to which they feel comfortable in a particular organisation and able to work within the dominant culture. This can be illustrated by making use of examples from journalism. Lloyd (2004) claims that journalists are invariably influenced by the culture, moral positions and assumptions held by their own news organisations. This newsroom culture evolves over time and constantly renews itself. It helps journalists to locate what is newsworthy and influences the way they respond to particular events or issues. In order for events or issues to appear newsworthy, journalists often look for what is novel, dramatic and sexually charged. These characteristics are valued above things that are overgeneralised, impersonal or dull (see Carrabine, 2008). The dominant culture in a newsroom will help to set the tone expected in reports and transmit a particular ideology of journalism; though this can leave journalists struggling to reconcile the expectations of their employer with their own sense of what is right.

Corporate culture

The corporate culture identifies how work should be approached in a particular organisation. Although this can sometimes be imposed from above, there is often room for it to develop from the working practice of people within an organisation and as such '. . . it grows organically and without plan or strategy' (Templar, 2003, p. 112). Svendsen (2008) notes that workers are increasingly expected to '. . . internalize the corporate culture, and embody the company's values and spirit' (p. 82). Organisations have a vested interest in creating a sense of common purpose amongst their workers. They can attempt to do this by finding ways to spread corporate values and by attempting to forge a corporate identity. Svendsen (2008) notes how this applies in particular to white-collar workers who are called upon to feed the needs of corporations by transferring their knowledge to corporate sites for distribution amongst the workforce. At the same time as expecting people to be creative and innovative, there is a definite emphasis upon harnessing the talents of workers and inculcating a team spirit to help direct their activities (Svendsen, 2008). Corporations become living beings with their own needs. Their characters are defined by a value system, a brand and by the knowledge created by workers and transferred in the interests of corporate progress.

A worker's knowledge and awareness of the corporate culture will often depend upon their place in the hierarchy. Kolb (1984) claims that professions have particular cultures which influence the approach taken by their workers and that '. . . one becomes a member of a reference group of peers who share a professional mentality, a common set of values and beliefs about how one should behave professionally' (Kolb, 1984, p. 88). Workers who seek to rise through the ranks of management often find that their identities are transformed in the process. In the professions, those who move on to managerial work find that the knowledge base of their work as a professional becomes less important than the move '. . . towards more managerial practices, based on strategy, direction setting and performance management' (Tomlinson, 2013, p. 51). The values associated with particular professions are embedded within corporate cultures. They help to orientate individual workers and influence the relationships between colleagues. When those who move on to senior management become preoccupied with strategy, they may well find themselves developing initiatives within the framework set by the existing corporate culture, even if they intend to transform this culture and enhance the professional values of the workforce.

It is possible for workers to look upon corporate culture as a context for their own development at work. Fox (2006) notes that workers who identify strongly with the aims and ethos of their organisation will tend to be willing to work over and above their contractual obligations, defend and promote the aims of their organisation and are likely to experience far higher levels of fulfilment at work. This fulfilment will also make them more likely to build their careers in this organisation rather than look for alternative career paths. Organisations can help to enhance the commitment of their workers through building a sense of collective identity. This can be done by pointing to the unique features of the organisation as compared with rival groups and by convincing workers of the relatively high status of their organisation. Inspirational management can help secure the loyalty and cooperation of workers as long as their vision and the promises made are delivered in an appropriate way, though managers who claim to be inclusive with the sole intention of securing compliance will often fail to convince workers of the importance of collective identity (see Fox, 2006). Corporate culture can be used to energise workers by embedding within their imaginations a direct link between the values of the organisation and their fulfilment at work. This does not, however, always have the desired effect (see box 2b).

2b: Students on corporate values

The promotion of corporate values can have a detrimental impact upon workers, especially those who have junior positions in an organisation. Terry noted that the handing down of such values by privileged management made him and many of his colleagues '. . . feel even more helpless and irrelevant within our jobs' (Terry). In his view, managers found ways to ignore the feedback they were given and often dismissed constructive suggestions from junior staff '. . . as though my personal merit and worth has already been judged simply because of the scale of our pay difference' (Terry). Corporate values might be designed to unite and to give direction to workers in an organisation, but these can easily become a source of resentment.

Shaping the work culture and the search for commitment

The work culture can have a dramatic effect upon the ways in which people view their identity as workers and will inevitably change over time. The introduction of new workers will influence the dynamics within teams and will be of constant concern to employers and managers. Employers have a vested interest in securing the commitment of their workers, though the extent of the commitment required will differ between occupations and will vary on a continuum, including a commitment to turn up and perform mundane tasks to the need to engage in continuing professional development. In attempting to shape the work culture, managers will often look for workers who hold certain values and display certain characteristics. Research on the retail sector, for example, has shown that employers are particularly interested in workers who are able to adopt an entrepreneurial approach to their work and recognise the importance of being proactive and customer-focused (Tomlinson, 2013). Some employers have definite types of people in mind for their organisation. Richard Branson (2008) claims there is a certain type of person who can thrive at Virgin. This is somebody who is friendly, open and smart regardless of formal education. He claims that the Virgin group is particularly interested in '. . . people who can grow into their work, and respond with excitement when we give them greater responsibility' (Branson, 2008, p. 19). In this sector, it would seem that youthful enthusiasm is valued very highly. It is not simply a matter of having workers who can perform their functions, but of having people who can express their personalities and project their finer qualities to customers. We will deal with some of the implications of this later in this chapter when we turn to look at the nature and significance of emotional labour.

Work and leisure

The blurring of boundaries between work and leisure can also have an important influence on the way work is viewed. For many people, work is a shared experience rather than something conducted in isolation of others. The extent to which workers are dependent upon each other will differ and this could be a key factor in determining how they conceptualise the relationship between their work and leisure. In isolated communities of workers (for example, miners and loggers), members of the workforce will tend to associate with each other during their leisure time. This is thought to help forge a common identity (Watson, 2003). In less extreme working environments, workers will often have a choice of who to befriend and how to spend their leisure time. This in turn will influence the way they see themselves and their colleagues (see box 2c).

learning about work

2c: Students on work and leisure

Students have noted how the emotional bonds created at work impact upon their sense of identity to a far greater extent than the job itself (Connie). Through working long hours in a busy hotel, Elizabeth found that she socialised with colleagues after her shift because of the unsociable hours they spent at work and because she found it helpful to socialise with those who understood the stress she encountered at work. She said, moreover, that it can become '. . . difficult to spend time with friends in other employment as your work patterns are so completely different' (Elizabeth). Socialising with colleagues can have its drawbacks. Beth found that she began to fear that any comments she made about work would find their way back to management, and she would suffer as a consequence. Unable to trust her colleagues, she began to withdraw and became unhappy at work (Beth). These comments illustrate how the atmosphere and demands of work can either draw colleagues together or create distance between them and that contentment at work is often linked to finding the right balance between isolation and integration in the work setting.

In order to understand the importance of work for individual identity, it is important to shatter some of the illusions about the permanence of jobs and the solidity of individual identity. Although it is no doubt possible to see how work influences the way that people see themselves, it is important to realise that individuals are rarely locked into a single identity. Instead, individuals thrash around looking for places to belong. When they are lucky enough to find these places, they begin to process what is expected of them and what they need to do in order to perform their tasks and survive in the work setting. The theoretical perspectives outlined earlier provide different ways to conceptualise the link between work and identity. They draw attention to the importance of work for intrinsic satisfaction as well as material rewards. They show that the search for pleasure, self-worth and an evolving sense of self will influence the way that individuals approach work and the escape routes they design for themselves. Using these theoretical frameworks, it is possible to see that work becomes something that individuals can use to reshape their lives. Rather than seeing workers as people who have to fit the needs of employers, it is also possible to see that workers can use work to construct their own sense of self and to determine how they interact with others in the work setting and beyond. These theoretical perspectives do, however, rely heavily upon individuals having an interest in the work they do and the desire to move on and prosper in their own way. They rest upon the assumption that people want to be autonomous, empowered and kinetic in their approach to work. They attempt to drag us away from seeing the work process as something that is imposed upon individuals who accept its constraints without thought and devoid of any view of themselves as evolving beings. The theories outlined so far do not, moreover, provide us with a way to understand *how* work helps to construct the ways in which people think and feel about themselves. Taking a look at the process of socialisation at work should help to provide an additional way to conceptualise the influence of work upon individual identity and to dig a little deeper into some of the fluctuations in the way people see themselves.

Socialisation at work

Workers are socialised into their jobs and have to find a way of reconciling this with the way they view themselves. The socialisation process not only inducts you into a specific job, it also helps you to acclimatise to a particular organisation and perhaps to a specific sector of employment. Individual identity is influenced in this way because workers begin '. . . to understand themselves as an employee, but also their legitimacy and acceptance as members of a work organisation' (Tomlinson, 2013, p. 124). The ability to work for a particular employer depends not only upon having the right skills, attitude and experience but also upon recognising that taking on a particular job transforms your status. Workers become visible and are often scrutinised by management and colleagues in terms of their ability to perform tasks and cooperate with others. Although this transformation can take place over prolonged periods, workers are expected to pick up the skills necessary for work and the attitudes necessary to solidify their presence as rapidly as possible.

Occupational groups will have distinctive ways to induct new members into the values of a particular occupation or profession. Watson (2003) provides examples from two professions to illustrate this process. Although there are notable differences between training to be a doctor and learning to be a prostitute, he argues that there are considerable similarities in the socialisation process. He notes that medical students combat relatively low status by adopting cynical attitudes associated more closely with the student culture. These values change, however, as they approach graduation when they start to embrace the professional values associated with the medical profession. Watson also looked at how prostitutes develop a value system to make sense of the work they do. This value system rests upon a belief that humans are corrupt, their customers are 'marks' worthy of being fleeced and that they need to secure the maximum gain for the minimum of effort. These values are thought to be necessary in order for prostitutes to maintain their own self-respect. Prostitutes are thought to create barriers between themselves and their clients, avoid emotional entanglements and often adopt an alter ego. This might involve prostitutes seeing themselves as skilled educators (see Watson, 2003). The illustrations provided by Watson show how the adoption of a new value system is essential for both professions and that, in very different ways, these values can help to elevate the status of new workers, prepare them for the demands of their work and create some common ground with their colleagues and peers. The way these values are transmitted will no doubt differ. Whilst the values needed to survive in the sex industry might be passed on by experienced workers in a deliberate way, it is quite possible that student doctors are expected to soak up appropriate values and make use of their own powers of observation. Either way, these illustrations can be used to show how workers new to an industry or profession can become acquainted with the necessary values and approach to work.

2d: Students on socialisation and inductions

New workers are often provided with a formal induction when they join an organisation. A formal tour around the working environment and some brief introductions to other workers helped Ben to overcome the feeling that he was an outsider (Ben). Formal inductions can, however, be counterproductive. One student noted that his induction consisted of a corporate brief which covered the business aims of the organisation. This made him feel insignificant and nothing more than a 'small cog in the big machine' (Miles). It is worth remembering that in addition to being inducted at work, those who do the induction are also influenced by the process. Giving somebody the responsibility to guide new workers and explain the rules of the game can enhance their own sense of identity at work. Tanya felt that this '. . . offered me a more powerful identity, allowing others to see me as a role model' (Tanya). Although formal inductions are only part of the socialisation process at work, these inductions can be very important in providing new workers with their first impressions of an organisation. More often than not, they will provide an insight into what management expects, which over time may be supplemented by the opinions and advice offered by colleagues.

Socialisation in journalism

As part of the socialisation process, workers need to learn the values associated with their profession and find ways to fit in. This can often involve taking on low-level tasks until they have established themselves and shown their willingness to learn and progress. In their research on communities of practice within a TV company, Grugulis and Stoyanova (2011) argued that important learning takes place within self-selected groups and through prolonged periods of socialisation. They discovered that workers were expected to learn through observation before moving on to assist experts and finally make the transition to work in specialist roles. In this industry, newcomers were assigned routine administrative tasks and had to learn the industry from scratch before they could be trusted to take on more responsibility (Grugulis and Stoyanova, 2011). Once they are given a break, junior staff might be reluctant to reveal their need for guidance and thereby subject themselves to a difficult period of transition. BBC journalist Kate Adie (2002) recalled that she had no formal training as a journalist and made fundamental errors in the early stages of her career. She had to learn the ways television news items were constructed and how to compress her commentary into a small amount of time. She talked about bluffing her way through interviews and feeling like a fraud. She had no time or opportunity to observe other journalists at work, and this created problems for her. She therefore picked up pieces of information wherever she could and realised she would have to learn through her mistakes. Although her camera crew would sometimes provide her with some helpful advice, more often than not she would have to improvise as best she could and develop her own particular way of reporting the news. Whilst illustrating the importance of being flexible and being willing to take advantage of opportunities as they present themselves, these examples from journalism also reveal some of the power dynamics involved in the socialisation process. New employees will inevitably have to find their place in an organisation and learn who they can trust to provide useful advice and guidance. These alliances can be particularly important in deflecting the obstacles planted by cliques.

Changing conditions of work and identity

The attempt to trace how individuals are influenced by the work they do has focused so far upon an individual moving into an organisation from the outside and the socialisation process involved in aiding this transition. It is worth considering, however, that the nature of work within a particular organisation will also change and that workers will be expected to adapt. Changes in working conditions can sometimes have a dramatic impact upon a worker's sense of identity. Pritchard and Symon (2011) conducted a series of interviews with human resource workers who took on the role of advisers in a call centre setting. These advisers believed in the first instance that their professional identity was under threat, partly because their role in the call centre was deemed to be of limited significance by colleagues in the human resource profession. The interviews showed, however, that the advisers soon began to develop a new sense of professional identity which highlighted the other skills they developed in the new setting. In particular, they said they were engaged in problem solving and in finding ways to communicate effectively with their client group. Rather than seeing themselves as providing information, these advisers took on a counselling role in many instances and began to see the importance of their role in providing the necessary support for their clients. Increasingly, they emphasised the human element of their work and constructed a view of themselves as frontline advocates defending and advancing the welfare of other workers. This research shows how workers can bounce back from apparent reductions in their status to reassess their professional identities and salvage what they can from changes in their working conditions.

The character of work within a particular organisation or sector of employment will also be influenced by the social composition of the workforce. Some sectors have been transformed by the influx of middle-class workers into fairly menial jobs. In the hotel and hospitality trade, for example, employers have showed a preference for hiring people based upon their looks, cultural capital and class background. The widespread availability of students seeking employment has tended to provide employers looking to enhance the aesthetic tone of their hotels and restaurants with a pool of relatively cheap and flexible labour. As a result, codes of civility traditionally associated with these sectors have been transformed. Middle-class students filled with self-belief and the conviction that they are en route to higher qualifications and professional jobs refuse to adopt subordinate characteristics (Warhurst and Nickson, 2007). In this instance, the identity and value system of young middle-class workers has helped to change the hotel and restaurant trade. This is important in showing a reciprocal element of the socialisation process. In addition to providing workers with a sense of the values and skills needed in their job, workers are also in a position to exert their own influence on the character of a particular organisation or sector. This might be through refusing to abide by the values transmitted by management and can take place as a result of the influence of small groups within the workplace. The cultures associated with particular professions do change, and these shifts in approach do not necessarily reflect the vision of senior management.

We have seen that the socialisation process at work plays an important part in the transition of workers either into new jobs or into new roles. This process is essential in making dominant values explicit and transferable and then helping to bestow changes in status upon workers. It can be seen as a shorthand method to consider the ways in which people learn about work. Examples from journalism, the medical profession and even the sex industry can be used to illustrate some of the features of this important learning process. We have seen, moreover, that the socialisation process goes beyond the induction of new workers and continues to exert an influence upon professional development as workers move through organisations. People are socialised by the overt corporate messages of organisations and, more importantly, by their closest colleagues. It is from these people that new workers gain an insight into the reality of working for a particular employer and even some tips on how to fit in to the groups already existing. It is important to note that this form of colleague-to-colleague socialisation provides workers with a means to exert their influence. They can teach their colleagues important lessons but also chip away at the dominant value system and modify it over time to reflect some of their own experiences. In some cases, this can mean drawing a line under past conventions and ushering in new approaches to work.

Emotional labour

The literature on emotional labour tends to be anchored in the writings of Arlie Hochschild, whose classic study *The Managed Heart* (2012) showed that workers in the service industry are often expected to display a limited selection of positive emotions. Her research, conducted with flight attendants for Delta airlines in the United States, revealed the damage that can be caused when the emotions of workers are supervised and micromanaged and when workers are expected to suppress the way they truly feel. In particular, workers can become anxious, stressed and alienated from themselves. She notes that although the ability to act and to display appropriate emotions can become a resource for workers, it can also be exploited by employers and thus become a site of struggle for people as they attempt to censor their emotions in a work setting.

Emotional labour involves individuals managing their emotions in a pre-determined way in the interest of the employer (Rogers, Creed and Searle, 2014). Workers are sometimes inducted or trained to express a particular demeanour and to display those emotions considered consistent with and necessary for a particular role (Watson, 2012). Zorn (2003) identifies three ways in which emotions can be used to promote the interests of employers. Emotions can be expressed to encourage customers to buy various products and services. Emotions can also be used by management to secure greater compliance and to enhance the commitment of workers to the strategic aims of the employer. Finally, emotions can serve to link workers and their clients. Workers can encounter emotional problems because they are suppressing their true feelings and projecting a fake persona. The existence and display of authentic feelings is central to one's own identity, unlike the emotions deliberately expressed in a professional setting (see Mann, 1997). The nature of emotional labour is thus twofold in that it involves not only the projection of prescribed emotions but also involves the workers in emotional wear and tear as they suppress who they are and take on another persona.

Emotional labour relies upon the ability of people to act and to project an emotion regardless of how they feel. Hochschild (2012) distinguished between surface acting and deep acting. Surface acting is where the emotion is put on or simulated, whilst deep acting is where individuals work on their own feelings and how to express them. Rogers et al. (2014) notes that surface acting is where a person pretends to feel a certain way and expresses this to the client. They argue that the expression of insincere emotions rarely has the desired effect and can alienate a client group. In order to develop deep acting, workers need to reassess their thoughts and feelings so as to develop their emotions and express these authentically. In their view, the cultivation of sincere emotions is far more likely to produce a favourable response from clients. The research conducted by Rogers et al. showed that doctors who relied upon surface acting and upon expressing inauthentic emotions were prone to burnout. Conversely, doctors who engaged in deep acting by cultivating suitable emotions experienced less tension at work and became far more robust. It should be noted, however, that the relative value of surface acting and deep acting will vary across sectors of employment. Part of this could be attributed to the different expectations placed upon workers in the professions.

Emotional labour and the professions

The character of the professions can be heavily influenced by the emotional labour cultivated and expected in each particular sector. According to Watson (2012), workers involved in emotional labour are expected to display a professional demeanour that conceals negative emotions, but these emotions can break through at times. People might attempt to manage their emotions by adhering to social conventions or by deferring to the expectations outlined in professional codes of conduct (Watson, 2012). Emotional labour involves not only the expression of particular emotions but also the suppression of less desirable emotional states. In the professions, managers will often encourage their staff to limit the range of emotions they display in front of their client group (Zorn, 2003). Mann (1997) claims that emotional detachment can be an important part of professional demeanour and that middle managers in the professions are often encouraged to conceal their emotions and present a crackless face to their workers. Emotional labour might involve, therefore, the expression of valued emotions through smiling and through the skilful use of body language but can also create barriers between workers, especially where the alternative is to express frustration and hostility. The use of emotional labour in the professions can be illustrated further with examples from teaching and from the police service.

Emotional labour and teaching

Those involved in teaching not only transmit a particular body of knowledge but are also involved in a series of emotional relationships or transactions with their students. Chowdhry (2014) showed how female, further-education lecturers in Scotland often found that they were being expected to deal with the emotional needs of their students to a far greater extent than their male counterparts. Students returning to learning in the further-education sector often have complex emotional and social needs and commitments outside of their studies that need to be taken into account and negotiated with teaching staff. This nurturing role can have a detrimental impact upon women lecturers in particular, who take this on above their workload. Tensions can arise, moreover, where the lecturers are teaching a formal curriculum in health and social care and are expected to apply the same values in their pastoral roles because '. . . the altruistic internalised care values of the care lecturers may provide a means for the exploitation of their emotional labour in the facilitation of college policies aiming to provide support to students with complex needs' (Chowdhry, 2014, p. 569). This research is important in showing how emotional labour can ripple through different layers within work. The lecturers involved in the study were put under pressure by their academic discipline, the college and by gender stereotypes to work and interact with students in a particular way. It was apparent that the lecturers became frustrated because this important dimension of their work often went unnoticed and was rarely expressed within their formal workloads.

Emotional labour and police

Police officers, who might be expected to respond to a multitude of conflicting events and emotions in a single shift, are also involved in emotional labour. According to Schaible and Gecas (2010), the spread of community policing and the redesign of police work has created some confusion about the role of police officers. Whilst police officers might be inducted into the new values of community policing, this does not mean that these values are shared by their colleagues who might hold on to a different view of policing. A survey of 109 police officers in an American police department revealed that problems can arise because police officers are expected to display a limited range of behaviours and suppress their immediate emotions. The ability to empathise and to display appropriate emotions is valued highly in the modern police service, but the response of police officers in the survey showed that the ability to distance themselves from the horrors of their work and to display surface emotions was considered essential for their own emotional well-being. Officers claimed that those who were unable to make effective use of such defence mechanisms were likely to encounter the problems of burnout and emotional exhaustion. This research shows how surface acting can be particularly important to police officers and can help them to deal with some of the demands of their work. This is in total contrast to the example used earlier about the emotional demands of being a doctor, where the ability to engage in deep acting was considered essential. Whilst it is clear that the police officers surveyed would advise their colleagues to protect themselves by keeping a lid on their emotions, one can only surmise that this was because of the need to deal with challenging behaviour on a regular basis.

By looking at emotional labour, it is possible to reveal some of the hidden dimensions of work and to recognise the enduring impact of emotional socialisation. It is worth looking at emotional labour in different sectors of employment to see its relative importance and to gain some appreciation of the ways in which workers can become divorced from their finer feelings because of the official sanctioning of particular ways of being. There are, however, numerous traps awaiting researchers who have an interest in the cultivation of emotions amongst workers. It would be wrong to assume that all workers feel the same strain on their identities and that all of these finer emotions are false and cultivated solely in the interest of employers. Difficulties will arise in defining emotions, comparing how individuals experience these emotions and determining to what extent individual workers are surface acting, deep acting or indeed expressing emotions that come easy to them. Being able to express these emotions could be fulfilling as well as an alienating process. We will move on to consider the relationship between alienation and fulfilment in more detail in the next chapter.

Conclusion

We have started to unpack some of the ways identities are formed through work and have seen the importance of interactions with colleagues and the need to learn some of the unspoken rules of work. Workers might need to go through this process a number of times, especially given the instability in the job market. By entering into a work culture, people work within a context for their own development. The values enshrined within this culture are transmitted through a process of socialisation, which helps people prepare for the work they do. We should bear in mind, however, that this work culture is by no means stable and will certainly change over time. Being in possession of the skills and values necessary to work effectively in a particular job might equip workers in the short term but will not sustain a worker for his or her entire career. Workers need to develop in order to survive the demands placed upon them at work. Whilst some of these demands can be resisted (see chapter 5), others will become enshrined within the dominant values of the organisations and thereby exert pressure on those who are seen as being out of step. By looking at the issue of emotional labour, we have seen that this process of socialisation can slice into the hearts of workers. In many ways, learning how to process their emotions and protect themselves on an emotional level is an essential part of the socialisation process at work and might even be more important than some of the skills needed in a particular job. As we move on to look at alienation and fulfilment, we will have another opportunity to investigate how people make sense of the work they do and judge its impact upon their own well-being.

Questions to consider

Making use of your own experience of work, consider the following:

1. How has work influenced the way you see yourself?
2. To what extent does the socialisation you receive at work undermine your autonomy and distinctiveness?
3. To what extent does your employer exert pressure on you to express positive emotions?

A guide to reading

Interesting introductions to the issues of identity, socialisation and emotional labour can be found in Watson (2003 and 2012) and in Macintosh and Mooney (2000). These topics can also be approached by making use of the key theoretical works of Bauman (1998; 2000; 2005), Beck (2000), de Botton (2009), Hochschild (2012) and Svendsen (2008). For those interested in examples from sectors of employment, the service industry is covered by Warhurst and Nickson (2007) and, from a managerial perspective, the work of Richard Branson (2008) can be illuminating. For examples from teaching, the work of Chowdhry (2014) explores a detailed case study of further education lecturers. Police work is covered in Schaible and Gecas (2010), whilst the stresses and strains on the identity and well-being of doctors can be found in Rogers et al. (2014).

References

Adie, K. (2002) *The Kindness of Strangers*, Headline Book Publishing: London.
Bauman, Z. (1998) *Globalization: The Human Consequences*, Polity: Cambridge.
Bauman, Z. (2000) *Liquid Modernity*, Polity: Cambridge.
Bauman, Z. (2005) *Work, Consumerism and the New Poor*, Open University Press: New York.
Beck, U. (2000) *The Brave New World of Work*, Polity Press: Cambridge.
Branson, R. (2008) *Business Stripped Bare*, Virgin Books: London.
Carrabine, E. (2008) *Crime, Culture and the Media*, Polity: Cambridge.
Chowdhry, S. (2014) 'The caring performance and the blooming student: Exploring the emotional labour of further education lecturers in *Scotland*', *Journal of Vocational Education & Training*, Volume 66, Issue 4, pp. 554–571.

Coats, D. and Max, C. (2005) *Healthy work: Productive workplaces*, The Work Foundation, The London Health Commission, http://www.theworkfoundation.com/assets/docs/publications/77_Healthy%20Work.pdf (last accessed 17.06.2014).

de Botton, A. (2009) *The Pleasures and Sorrows of Work*, Hamish Hamilton: London.

Dight, C. (2007) 'The key to wellbeing at work', *The Times*, 27 March 2007, p. 8.

Fox, C (2006) 'Truly, madly, cheaply?', *Australian Financial Review*, 10 November 2006, p. 68.

Grugulis, I. and Stoyanova, D. (2011) 'The missing middle: Communities of practice in a freelance labour market', *Work, Employment & Society*, Volume 25, Issue 2, pp. 342–351.

Hochschild, A. (2012) *The Managed Heart*, University of California Press: Berkeley.

Kolb, D. (1984) *Experiential Learning: Experience As a Source of Learning and Development*, Prentice Hall: New Jersey.

Lloyd, J (2004) *What the Media Are Doing to Our Politics*, Constable: London.

Macintosh, M. and Mooney, G. (2000) 'Identity, inequality and social class'. In K. Woodward (2000) *Questioning Identity: Gender, Class, Nation*, Routledge: London, pp. 79–114.

Mann, S. (1997) 'Emotional labour in organizations', *Leadership and Organization Development Journal*, Volume 18, Issue 1, pp. 4–12.

Pritchard, K. and Symon, G. (2011) 'Identity on the line: Constructing professional identity in an HR call centre', *Work, Employment & Society*, Volume 25, Issue 34, pp. 434–450.

Rogers, M., Creed, P., Searle, J. (2014) 'Emotional labour, training stress, burnout, and depressive symptoms in junior doctors', *Journal of Vocational Education & Training*, Volume 66, Issue 2, pp. 232–248.

Schaible, L. and Gecas, V. (2010) 'The impact of emotional labour and value dissonance on burnout among police officers', *Police Quarterly*, Volume 13, pp. 316–341.

Svendsen, L (2008) *Work*, Acumen: Durham.

Taylor, G. and Spencer, S. (2004) 'Introduction'. In G. Taylor and S. Spencer (eds) *Social Identity: Multidisciplinary Approaches*, Routledge: London, pp. 1–13.

Templar, R. (2003) *The Rules of Work*, Pearson: Harlow.

Tomlinson, M. (2013) *Education, Work and Identity*, Bloomsbury: London.

Warhurst, C. and Nickson, D. (2007) 'A new labour aristocracy: Aesthetic labour and routine interactive service', *Work, Employment & Society*, Volume 21, Issue 4, pp. 785–798.

Watson, T. (2003) *Sociology, Work and Industry*, Routledge: London, 2003 (4th edition).

Watson, T. (2012) *Sociology, Work and Organisation*, Routledge: Oxon.

Zorn, T. (2003) 'The emotionality of information and communication technology implementation', *Journal of Communication Management*, Volume 7, pp. 160–171.

chapter 3

Alienation, Fulfilment and the Working Environment

We have seen that work can have a dramatic impact upon the way people see themselves and that they might use work to enhance their own sense of identity. If everybody had the qualifications, the aptitudes and the experience necessary to do what they want in the way they choose, there could be harmony between their sense of identity and their work. People would be able to choose jobs to suit their abilities and aspirations and the job in turn could reinforce their sense of self. The problem, however, is that work is not always enriching. Work can sometimes undermine confidence and deprive people of satisfaction and fulfilment. When this occurs, we talk about being or feeling alienated. Workers can find themselves caught between two distinct inner states. The internal goods created by work can lift and inspire the worker to work with passion and innovation. Work can also make them feel wretched, exhausted and unfulfilled and perhaps instil within them the belief that the more they work the more foolish they become. Exploited and stripped of his or her finer qualities, the alienated worker lives in dread of work and desperate for diversion. Alienation and fulfilment can be seen as a framework within which many workers operate. The way they locate themselves within this framework can reveal a great deal about their expectations of work and their assumptions about the rewards of work. By taking these two concepts into account, people might be better placed to make informed decisions about their work and the way they conceptualise the development of their careers. Alienation and fulfilment are not merely passive descriptions of the way individuals feel about work, but they are also tools they can use to make important decisions about the work they do and the way they want to develop. In addition to viewing alienation and fulfilment as inner states stemming from the way workers look upon the work they do and how this fits with their own identity, it is important to recognise that individuals are also influenced by the environments within which they live and work. In order to examine this, we will take a closer look at some of the arguments presented for and against open-plan offices.

Alienation

Work can have a devastating effect upon an individual's sense of identity. When it does, we talk about workers experiencing alienation. The classic account of alienation can be found in Marx's *Economic and Philosophical Manuscripts* (Marx, 1844), where he attempted to show how inhumane economic systems strip people of their finer qualities. Capitalism is said to deny workers of a means to express themselves through their work by depriving workers of the product of their labour and, in so doing, contaminate their characters and social relations. According to Marx, alienation cannot be overcome simply by raising wages but relies upon the abolition of private property. This would enable workers to reconnect with their true selves. Because alienation affects all strata of society, Marx believed that the emancipation of the workers would liberate society as a whole. In addition to abolishing private property, production would have to be made an arena of human creativity and self-expression (see Marx, 1844). Marx did not deny that work in itself could be a means for individuals to express and fulfil themselves, only that work under capitalism denied individuals the freedom and creativity necessary for this to occur. This is shown in *The German Ideology* (1845) where Marx and Engels outlined their vision of communism, which relied heavily upon workers exploring their creative sides and engaging in a variety of occupations rather than being confined to a single specialism demanded by the capitalist system. Indeed, Marx and Engels said that a communist system would make it possible for the individual to '. . . hunt in the morning, fish in the afternoon, rear cattle in the evening, criticise after dinner, just as I have a mind, without ever becoming hunter, fisherman, herdsman or critic' (Marx and Engels, 1845, p. 54). This freedom was deemed essential for workers to move beyond the alienated state experienced under capitalism. Whilst capitalism was thought to eat away at workers, an alternative economic system would allow for work to become what it should be. For those who follow this line of argument, work should be a means to fulfilment and a way for workers to connect with their true selves. It should be noted, however, that this view of the possibilities of work rests upon a firm belief that work has a determining effect upon individual identity, rather than the argument that work is one of many influences upon the identity of the individual. It also speculates on the benefits of variety in work and that this variety is prevented by the demands of the capitalist system. What this does not recognise sufficiently is that workers might choose to specialise and to remain in their comfort zones.

Alienation and the search for diversion

If work deprives workers of fulfilment and becomes an oppressive force within their lives, then it is likely they will find ways to distance themselves from work and enter into their own worlds to protect themselves from the detrimental impact of the work they do. Boredom can have a corrosive effect upon workers and convince them that their true happiness lies outside of work. Svendsen (2008) claims that boredom at work stems not from having too little to do but from an inability to attribute meaning to work. If this occurs, people can find themselves suffering at work because work becomes a burden (Svendsen, 2008). Alienation does not, however, have to be seen simply as the absence of fulfilment but can also be seen as the driving force behind aggressive, resistant and destructive behaviour. This can sometimes be channelled into the demand for constructive reform, but this is by no means the most likely scenario. Alain de Botton (2009) notes that modern work blunts the intelligence of people, stifles their creativity and pushes them towards destructive behaviour. The numerous fights that take place on Saturday nights can serve as a reminder '... of the price we pay for our daily submission at the alters of prudence and order – and of the rage that silently accumulates beneath a uniquely law-abiding and compliant surface' (de Botton, 2009, pp. 45–46). People are not soothed by alienating experiences. They confront them as dangerous and disruptive, but individuals still have a choice of how to respond. It could be that people shut down in order to protect their inner core, almost like a computer closing an application to protect itself from an incoming virus. Alternatively, alienation can chisel away at inner peace and stability, stir the emotions and erupt through anger. Either way, work can be viewed as a source of misery and dissatisfaction.

3a: Students on alienation at work

Low-paid, low-skilled and monotonous work can be very disempowering. Wes reflected upon his own experience working on tills during long shifts. He claimed that he despised this work, felt an acute sense of estrangement and that he regarded his supervisor at work as an 'agent of capitalism'. For Wes, this work could provide nothing more than a wage and he felt that the monotony and lack of control was alienating (Wes).

Downsizing, redesign and the pace of work

Satisfaction in work can also be damaged by downsizing, the redesign of jobs and the pace of work. The process of downsizing encourages the belief that more can be done by fewer workers as long as more efficient ways of working can be introduced. It is estimated that in the United States, approximately 39 million jobs were downsized in the period 1980–1995 (see Bauman, 2005). In a study based at a large manufacturing company in the United States, Greenberg and Grunberg (2003) attempted to judge the impact of downsizing and redesign upon attitudes towards work. They found that many workers who had experienced job loss remained anxious about the future and experienced low levels of satisfaction at work. However, employees who had survived downsizing were said to be more concerned that management had carried out the process fairly and reasonably and had provided workers with help to find new work. This tended to make the workers feel less uncertain about their own futures. Although the redesign of jobs can have negative effects for some employees who find rapid change and the need to learn new skills uncomfortable and threatening, some workers welcome job redesign and see it as a chance to learn new skills, avoid boredom and to work with different people. Research suggests (see Oswald, 2002) that satisfaction in work is often undermined by the unrealistic expectations of management. This applies in particular when tight deadlines are imposed from above without suitable consultation with workers. The studies outlined earlier illustrate that anxiety and dissatisfaction at work stem not only from the changing nature of a particular job but more often than not from management failing to communicate this effectively, consult workers in a constructive way and treat their employees with the respect they deserve.

Lack of career progression

Lack of career progression can also be alienating. According to research conducted by the training organisation Common Purpose (2004b), people are most likely to feel disillusioned with their jobs at the age of 30. This applies in particular when there are few challenges, a failure on the part of employers to offer development opportunities and help employees fulfil their potential and a seeming inability to advance beyond their current role and minimal opportunity to be creative and/or innovative. Of the people surveyed, 91% felt it was important for employers to recognise diverse points of view, as well as encourage people to express their opinions. When it came to career progression, 46% of respondents felt that management was too inflexible and that management did not have the interests of their workers as heart. For 47% of the people surveyed, hierarchical structures at work were thought to stifle opportunities for career progression. Failure to recognise the contribution made by individual workers and their potential to operate at a higher level can undermine fulfilment at work and cast a shadow over the work process for many workers. Although it could be argued that restricting opportunities for some workers is necessary because of deficits in their skills, it should be recognised that management will often have some responsibility for dampening the enthusiasm of the worker by failing to give credence to their desire to advance at work. Although all workers are by no means careerist, this does not mean they have no interest in having their work recognised and rewarded accordingly. Failure to take this into account can have long-term negative effects upon the attitude of workers and their fulfilment at work.

Neglect of ambition

Lack of fulfilment at work can arise when the values of an organisation do not correspond to those of their employees and when an organisation fails to appreciate the ambitions of its staff. According to Common Purpose (2004a), young managers are more likely to stay with an organisation when they can see congruence between their own values and those of their employer. In a survey of 200 junior and middle managers, over half of the sample reported feeling unfulfilled at work and were considering looking for a new position. In a separate study involving 1000 employees aged 25–35, Common Purpose (2004b) claimed that many young people experience a quarter-life crisis as they struggle to reconcile the need to work in order to pay off debts and their longing for more fulfilling employment. The vast majority of those questioned wanted a career to match their wider ambitions. For 82% of the sample, those organisations failing to accommodate the ambitions of their staff ran the risk of losing them. The research conducted by Common Purpose concentrated upon workers involved in the management of others and identifies a clear link between ambition and fulfilment for this group of staff. We should bear in mind, however, that there is an agenda behind this research. Groups like Common Purpose have an interest in identifying dissatisfaction at work and to drawing a connection between low levels of satisfaction and gaps in opportunities for training and career development. It is clear that such research focusses primarily upon the individual as a motivated agent of change. It does not take into account the impact of capitalist values, bureaucracy and dysfunctional teams upon levels of satisfaction in work but concentrates instead on what individuals can do to enhance their career prospects.

The detrimental impact of work

Expectations of work can play an important role in determining how people interpret their experiences and how they judge the impact of work on their sense of self and their own well-being. Each sector of employment will have its own challenges and its own rewards. For some sectors, insecurity is hard to avoid. In a survey by the union, Unite (2010), it was found that over 90% of voluntary sector staff believe that the lack of funding, the culture of cost cutting and short-term contracts undermine their sense of well-being. Voluntary sector workers recorded high levels of stress and anxiety and claim that many experienced staff leave the voluntary sector in search of more security. Other sectors of employment enjoy considerably higher levels of security, yet also experience high levels of dissatisfaction. The following accounts will draw upon the experiences of teachers, social workers and police officers.

Teaching

In 2001, the National Union of Teachers claimed that teachers leave the profession because of excessive workloads, poor pupil behaviour, stress-related illness and relatively low pay (National Union of Teachers, 2001). Illingworth (2007) identified the problems of long working hours, increased levels of bureaucracy associated with inspections and monitoring, disruptive pupils and the feeling that they had no control over their own working lives. Atkins, Carter and Nichol (2002) noted that '. . . teachers feel they have little or no control over their workloads. It is this lack of control not just the number of hours that leads to stress' (Atkins et al., 2002, p. 9). Teachers often find that in order to do their jobs properly, they are expected to do unpaid overtime. A TUC survey in 2010 noted that at least one in five teachers does 17 hours of unpaid overtime per week and that the majority do at least 10 hours overtime per week without any extra pay (TUC, 2010a). Part of this can be attributed to the hidden features of the job. Rothi, Leavey and Loewenthal (2010) noted that teachers will often have to do their paperwork during evenings and weekends because their attention is focused upon providing emotional and social support to pupils as well as teaching their particular subjects. The research noted earlier shows that teaching often involves high workloads that can eat into life outside of work and contribute towards unease, stress and a decline in general well-being. Whilst this could be seen as an unavoidable characteristic of this form of work, from a union perspective, the practice of relying upon workers doing unpaid overtime is clearly not acceptable.

Social work

Although social work training often contains a practical element, it is not possible to train a social worker to deal with all of the complexities associated with their career. Students completing a degree in social work are only at the beginning of their training (see Cartwright, 2007). The pressures on social workers can be extreme. Laurance (2008) notes how social workers often have to deal with intimidating families and client groups and have to manage an extremely high case load. Based upon her own experience as a social worker, Gaynor Arnold (2009) noted how social workers often have 20–30 complex cases open at any one point. The ability of social workers to communicate with difficult families can also pose problems if social workers lose focus on who they need to help. Arnold confesses that if she was a recent graduate it is unlikely that she would choose social work as a career because of the stress involved in working in the profession. Although she remained convinced of the importance of social work and maintains great respect for those in the profession, she felt it is important to manage expectations and strive to protect social workers from being blamed mercilessly for the mistakes they make under stressful circumstances. Social workers have, however, also noted how the difficulties and challenges of the job can be a source of excitement and fulfilment at work. Andy Bell (2005), a senior social worker at the Royal Alexandra Hospital for Sick Children, notes how his career is littered with minefields. He claims that, in order to survive, it is important that social workers have the ability to listen, make decisions and withstand hostility. He describes his job as '. . . interesting, exciting and very stressful – much like life really' (Bell, 2005, p.2). Whilst the stresses associated with social work will suit some people, it is clear that it is a challenging career and one where fulfilment might be difficult to find and sustain. In addition to having a client in need, social workers will also have to deal with families and carers who have their own perspective on the needs of the person and on the ability of social workers to make a positive contribution to their lives.

Police

The challenges of police work can have a dramatic effect upon the way police officers view themselves and others in the community. Joel Caplan (2003) worked for 12 months as a police officer in the United States and suggested that cynicism within the police force was a necessary tool to help police officers carry out their duties. According to Caplan, police officers are subjected to verbal and physical abuse from the public on a regular basis. In his view, this is compounded by public expectations of how the police should conduct themselves and by criticisms launched against the police by those who have little understanding of the job. He notes that even the most idealistic of police recruits find that their attitudes towards the community and their jobs become soured in '... an emotional tug-of-war between the public's affection and hostility' (Caplan, 2003, p.4). Although the development of cynicism can help some officers, it creates fundamental problems for those who enter the police force in the hope of serving the public and establishing a relationship based upon mutual respect. Caplan's recollections illustrate how workers can become bruised through their experience of a job and might need to reevaluate their career choices in light of the emotions experienced at work. It should be noted, however, that Caplan's comments on the attitudes of his colleagues illustrate that he regards cynicism as a barrier to effective police work and that his own motivations for leaving the police service were tied up with his view of himself and his fear that he would somehow become contaminated by his experiences and by the hostility shown by the community. Whereas many of his colleagues had learnt how to survive in a hostile environment, it is clear that he had struggled and had found that the job failed to live up to his expectations.

Meaningless work

The meaning people attribute to work and the way they regard the conditions of their employment can affect people in a multitude of ways. It is likely that an individual's health will suffer as soon as he or she regards the work they do as meaningless. Svendsen (2008) acknowledges that although there will be times when work swallows other aspects of life, there might be times when work will have virtually no meaning. During these times, people can become bored and struggle to function at work. Poor quality work can lead to lower levels of self-esteem, feelings of powerlessness, higher rates of mental illness and a diminished sense of well-being (see Coats and Max, 2005). Work could be said to be of poor quality when there is a lack of control over work and the environment in which work takes place, poor pay, excessive repetition, too much or too little work, long hours, a lack of respect from management and colleagues, bullying, poor line management, a lack of training and unsafe working conditions (see TUC, 2010b). When workers are unable to attribute meaning to their work, it becomes a means to an end at best and perhaps nothing more than a grind which depletes them as individuals and forces them to find distractions from their lives at work. This can be illustrated through student reflections (see box 3b).

This examination of alienation acknowledges that feelings of disenchantment at work stem from the way it is organised under a capitalist system. Work should not be viewed independently of its economic, social and polit-

3b: Students on poor quality work and the wearing of uniforms

When students attempt to characterise poor quality work, many of them talk about feeling alienated or disempowered when they are forced to wear a uniform at work. The wearing of a uniform can create unfortunate problems for young workers. One student claimed that it prevented her from being herself '. . . thus taking away aspects of my personal identity' (Sue). Hierarchies can be expressed in the clothes that workers are expected to wear. Lenny and his colleagues had to wear matching T-shirts whilst his supervisor was allowed to choose what clothes to wear. This made him feel at the bottom of the hierarchy and it did little to encourage hard work or respect for the management (Lenny). Low-skilled workers are often expected to wear uniforms. Miles recalled that his work selling popcorn in a large corporate cinema created problems for him if he was seen by people he knew outside of work because he would '. . . feel extremely embarrassed and it lowered my self-esteem' (Miles). He said that the uniform he had to wear '. . . stripped me of my personal identity and I became anonymous in the sense that everyone in the same uniform was a representative of the company' (Miles). He claimed, however, that he and his colleagues found ways to assert their individual identity by making slight changes to the way they wore their uniforms. Some of the workers would lift their collars on their shirts. Those with tattoos on their arms would roll their sleeves high enough to expose the least part of their tattoos. The workers were urged to include the name of their favourite film on their badges and this became '. . . the only legitimate means of putting across a personal trait or identity so people would pick films that they felt said as much about their identity as possible' (Miles). Whilst working conditions might be designed to standardise procedures and create a corporate image, this does not mean that all workers will comply with the expectations of management. As we will see in chapter 5, workers will find different ways to resist management and assert their own needs.

ical context. When Marx attempted to explore the reasons for alienation, he was careful to point out that capitalism, rather than work itself, was at fault. It is important to realise, moreover, that alienation affects society as well as the individual. Through the erosion of the worker's self-esteem, work under capitalism creates workers desperate for diversions and possibly hostile towards the community. Examples have been used from manufacturing and from middle management to show how workers are plagued by uncertainties and face obstacles for their own security and progression. It is worth bearing in mind, however, that this view of work is often based upon the belief that work should be fulfilling but that careers have been damaged in some way by poor organisation, bureaucracy and by dysfunctional individuals and pockets of society. The recollections of those who are disaffected by the career choice they have made provide one way of looking at work, which concentrates upon the limitations of work to satisfy the needs of the individuals concerned. Although they draw attention to the problems of stress and burnout, they also allude to coping mechanisms cultivated by some of their colleagues; and they acknowledge that their own interpretation of their experiences at work is not shared by all of their colleagues. Alienation has been identified as one end of a continuum which includes fulfilment.

Fulfilment

Work does not have to be a source of alienation. For many people, the search for fulfilling work is a prime motivational force in their lives. Svensden (2008) points out that approximately 30% of the contemporary American workforce belong to the 'creative class' and value their own individuality, creativity and distinctive qualities. This class of worker will tend to view work as a vocation and '. . . they are the ones who embody the romantic ideal of self-realization 24/7, and such realization is supposed to be the very essence of meaning in life' (Svendsen, 2008, p. 39). Whereas career choices used to say a lot about an individual and provide a person with a means of self-expression and even moral development, Bauman (2005) argues that work is increasingly judged primarily on aesthetic terms and '. . . by its capacity to generate pleasurable experience' (Bauman, 2005,p. 33). He claims that people want work that is interesting, fulfilling and varied. Such categories are valued highly in a society that emphasises the importance of the pleasure to be gained from consumption. Creativity is particularly important in the professions which emphasise training, continuous professional development and respect for the relative autonomy of professionals (see Hodson, 2001). Leaders at work are asked to convince workers that their work is essential for their self-realisation and is full of exciting opportunities. Workers are urged to 'upgrade' themselves. By taking note of what each employee has to offer and looking for signs that workers are seeking fulfilment in the work they do, managers and leaders are expected to harness the energy of individual workers for the good of the corporation (Svendsen, 2008). It should be noted that workers often look for fulfilment and are willing to sacrifice some material gains in order to secure this. Although it could be argued that capitalism deprives individuals of fulfilling work, this does not prevent individuals from attempting to cultivate the fulfilling aspects of their work. In order to make this even the remotest of possibilities, work under capitalism needs to be made more palatable.

Redressing the work-life balance

We have seen already that a poor work-life balance can increase stress at work and make work less fulfilling. From a union perspective (see TUC, 2010b), redressing the work-life balance would help to create a more fulfilled and healthy workforce and would benefit employers because people would take fewer days off sick. According to the Work Foundation (2008), paying serious attention to work-life balance can lead to increased productivity, greater recruitment and retention, lower rates of nonattendance and lead to a more satisfied workforce. For Jones (2003), people can gain more control over their working lives when they are allowed to make real choices about when, where and how they work. Whilst it is evident that workers have some responsibility for their own work-life balance, it also makes sense to place this onto the agenda for negotiations with employers. The evidence included earlier illustrates that redressing the work-life balance can benefit employees and employers and perhaps contribute towards increased fulfilment at work.

The importance of respect

Commanding respect at work is essential in the search for fulfilment. According to Coates and Lekhi (2008) '. . . an individual's desire to exercise a degree of autonomy in their work is an essential ingredient of self-respect' (Coates and Lekhi, 2008, p. 14). They claim that people remain citizens in the workplace and should have the same rights, for example, the rights to freedom of speech and freedom of association, as those they enjoy outside of the workplace. Work is a social act involving interaction between people, and workers have their own ambitions which may or may not match those of the organisation for which they work. Research conducted in Australia (see Hull and Read, 2003) found that good working relationships built upon trust, respect, self-worth and recognition were prioritised by workers and considered essential for a fulfilling work experience. Muirhead (2004) claims that attempting to control everything workers do will deplete them of energy and interest in their work, whilst allowing for greater levels of autonomy and recognising the humanity of labour can liberate individual skills and encourage workers to take on more responsibility. He believes that workers need to be challenged at work rather than reduced to perform simple repetitive tasks. Without these challenges, happiness and fulfilment at work can become more difficult to achieve and to sustain. The importance of respect should not be underestimated. Failure to recognise individual worth or neglect of basic civil rights will only serve to create distance between workers and their work. In order to challenge this, employers need to create an environment which acknowledges the rights of their workers. These rights go far beyond an economic transaction and should take into account the broader social needs of workers.

The lure of creativity

Those who are lucky enough to find work which exercises their creativity could find this is their gateway to fulfilment at work. Grigg and Lacey (2008) suggest that for many young people, work is no longer simply a job but an extension of their identities and values. Young graduates are particularly interested in work where they can be creative and innovative. According to Grigg (2008), companies have become aware of the need to offer graduates greater levels of autonomy and room to be creative. This could be through the way they are managed but also through providing finance to pump-prime projects and involve young recruits. Whilst money is still an important consideration for many employees, Grigg suggests that people are more concerned with working in a creative environment in which they have a reasonable degree of autonomy. The meaning of creativity will no doubt differ between sectors, but there would seem to be a consistent message here about the expectations of young workers in general and young graduates in particular. Although the promise of a decent salary might be enough to entice these people to take a job, it is not enough to sustain their interest and commitment to working for a particular employer. Room for creativity seems to be particularly important for graduates and for those who place a high value upon work as a means to fulfilment.

This creative urge is something that is embraced and celebrated by Richard Branson (2008), who claims that he was never really been interested in business for its own sake and had always seen it as a means to be creative. He talked about starting with a blank canvas, much like a visual artist, and attempting to create something new and exciting. For Branson, excitement is to be found in the vibrancy of a constantly evolving Virgin brand. He was also careful to point out that creativity in business relied upon gut instinct and making use of emotion rather than relying too much upon facts and figures. He noted with approval how Google employed people to be creative and to develop new ways of doing things and he believed that by '. . . giving their people ownership over their work in this way, the company and its customers have benefited enormously' (Branson, 2008, p. 219). But opportunities in the creative industries tend to be rather limited, and workers in these industries often find that much of their work is on short-term projects. Watson (2012) points out that although people might be drawn to these industries in the hope of providing an outlet for their creative and artistic abilities, the demands of the market also require them to take into account the business needs of the organisation. Because of this, they might find that they are torn between two opposing identities. Whilst individuals might be free to be as creative as they wish, this does not mean that there is a market for all forms of creativity. Although it might not be possible for many people to find work that matches their own creative impulses, this does not mean that there is no room to work in occupations with a creative dimension.

Good work

There have been numerous attempts to define the essential ingredients of a good job. The Commission on the Social Determinants of Health (2008) defined a good job as one that provides financial security, social status, personal development, beneficial social relationships and self-esteem. Coats and Lekhi (2008) believe that good jobs are secure, involve variation in tasks, some measure of autonomy, a balance between effort and reward and are where workers have the skills needed to deal with pressurised situations and strong workplace relationships. They suggest that government, employers and employees should take an interest in improving conditions of work. They claim, for example, that it is in the interest of employers to address the root causes of sick leave and to make improvements where possible to the working environment, the design of jobs and the performance of management. For the TUC (2010b) the quality of work depends upon the fair treatment of workers, the quality of management, the character of the work culture, the amount of job security and the physical and emotional demands of the job. These characterisations of good work look beyond the financial rewards of work and draw attention to the importance of security, variation, autonomy, respect and relationships at work. It is clear that people will vary in how they characterise good work and that workers will be motivated and inspired by a range of concerns (see box 3c).

3c. Students on the roots of good work

Students are often in low-skilled and low-paid jobs whilst they are studying for their degrees. They are, however, still able to find their work interesting and challenging. Working as a waiter, Alan found the challenge of adapting to the needs of his diverse customer base helped to keep the work interesting. Even fairly routine work in a financial department can provide opportunities for self-expression. Yana claimed that it 'put into action my creative side' and allowed her to '. . . reflect and re-evaluate myself and how effectively I was completing work tasks through my supervisor and work colleagues' reactions' (Yana). One student noted that tight deadlines at work had a positive impact on the way she saw herself and the way she managed conflicting demands upon her time. Apart from anything else, it allowed her to adopt a creative approach to work (Harriet). These reflections show that students can gain something from working in challenging environments and illustrate their commitment to their own development at work.

In looking at fulfilment in work, we have concentrated in the main on how workers might strive for variety, flexibility and stimulation in the work they do. We have seen how creativity can be important as a motivating force and how this can be linked to autonomy. The picture painted, however, is one of individuals attempting to nourish themselves through their work. This view of fulfilment does not take into account the economic, social and political barriers to fulfilment at work and does little more than entice workers to listen to their better selves in search of satisfaction and even self-realisation through the work they do. Whilst it is no doubt possible to crave and pursue creativity and to pay relatively little attention to the constraints imposed by the economic system, it is likely to remain an ideal for most people and one that can confront them as an alienating force. It is important, moreover, to recognise that ideas of creativity are socially constructed. Institutions and creative elites will determine the role of creativity in society and prescribe how far this can be accommodated within existing models of business. Although individuals might choose to distance themselves from work in order to pursue their own creative interests, the person seeking fulfilment in work will often have to mould their creative vision to the demands of the market or the needs of the employer. This might in itself be enough to convince people that true creativity is impossible to pursue within capitalist organisations. We now attempt to take this argument a little further by taking into account the impact of the working environment on the way workers view their work.

The working environment

Environmental psychologists (see Vischer, 2011) argue that the working environment is not passive but an active influence upon how people think, behave and work. Because the way workers experience the environment is influenced by the activities they perform, the relationship between workers and the environment is described as transactional. The working environment will have a major impact upon the emotional state of workers. Mazza (2008) claims that workers are influenced by both the physical dimensions of their environment and its emotional tone, both of which are said to impact upon the way workers view themselves and interact with colleagues. Whilst workers can be nourished by a warm and welcoming environment, they can also be made to feel isolated and alienated by the environment in which they work. Viewed in this light, alienation and fulfilment at work can be influenced by the design of workspaces. We will explore this in more detail by taking a look at some of the arguments for and against open-plan offices.

Arguments for open-plan offices

Open-plan offices can be beneficial to teams, especially when they use the space to assist in communication and to work on collective endeavours (see Vischer, 2011). Supporters of open-plan offices (see Rushton, 2013) point out the advantages of being able to meet people easily and to discuss work without having to plan additional times to meet. One commentator went so far as to say that '. . . walls between workers are the death knell for business communication' (Rushton, 2013, p. 2). The argument for open-plan offices owes a great deal to the development of online communities, but it has been noted that people '. . . failed to realise that what makes sense for the asynchronous, relatively anonymous interactions of the Internet might not work as well inside the face-to-face, politically charged, acoustically noisy confines of an open-plan office' (Cain, 2012, p. 79). The arguments for open-plan offices rest upon the idea that free-flowing communication between workers is useful and that people can develop far easier in this environment both individually and as members of a team. These arguments do not, however, take into account the importance of silence and solitude.

Arguments against open-plan offices

The journalist Jeremy Paxman (2014) pulled no punches when he called for a ban on open-plan offices. He condemned these environments as distracting health hazards and revealed what he considered to be the sinister reasons for arranging workspaces in this way. He claimed that open-plan offices were used to convince workers that they are dispensable and not valued intrinsically. Open-plan offices have been criticised because they allow for distractions (Vischer, 2011) and for the time it takes workers to regain concentration after being disturbed (Molloy, 2013). Stress levels tend to increase in open-plan offices because of poor design, especially when there is insufficient natural light and poor ventilation (Vischer, 2011). Individuals are thought to need their own space at work and to be able to define this territory and determine its use for themselves (Vischer, 2011). Rather than make workers more sociable and willing to share, open-plan offices have been shown to discourage people from opening up to their colleagues and to be more prone to becoming suspicious and guarded (Cain, 2012). The lack of personal space, indeed, can '. . . make workers feel insecure and aggressive, reducing their concentration span and lowering their productivity . . .' (Monaghan, 2009, p. 15).Open-plan offices have been shown to lead to a decline in productivity by creating a series of environmental distractions and problems, which in turn contribute towards increases in errors and in the time taken to complete work (Vischer, 2011). In a survey of computer programmers, it was found that the majority of those who were successful in their careers attributed this in part to having a good working environment and one which allowed them a reasonable amount of privacy and quiet space within which to work (Cain, 2012). Rather than improve communication between workers, open-plan offices are thought to intrude into the personal space needed by individuals, disrupt their thinking and encourage them to develop coping mechanisms to shut out the noise generated by their colleagues.

Flexible working environments

Even if places of employment are no longer willing to invest in private offices, there have been notable experiments in the use of flexible working environments. Susan Cain (2012) notes with approval the use of private offices with movable walls at Microsoft. This design allows for privacy and for a quiet workspace, whilst providing the possibilities of collaborative work when necessary. The animation studio Pixar has also been innovative in their design of their workspaces, which have included extensive communal areas, streets and amenities to encourage workers to socialise at work without disrupting their colleagues. It has been argued that an intelligent working environment is one that '. . . should be able to sense the interaction between users and space, process this information and understand the context data, react in a way that adjusts to users' needs and enhances their endeavours . . .' (Reijula, Grohn, Muller and Reijula, 2011, p. 234). Whilst open-plan offices might not do this, the use of flexible work environments which are changed depending upon the work carried out might provide an alternative.

It is evident that the working environment can have an impact upon levels of alienation or fulfilment at work, and this can be illustrated by reference to the arguments for and against open-plan offices. We have seen that supporters will defend open-plan offices because they can facilitate group working. This could be seen as an important source of fulfilment at work. Those who argue against open-plan offices draw attention to how individuals start to feel uncomfortable in their surroundings and shut down from their colleagues. This could in turn contribute towards feelings of alienation. What these arguments fail to take into account is the extent to which people use the spaces developed as intended. It is clear that open-plan offices were not designed to be distracting. Nor, it could be said, were they designed primarily to aid communication. Instead, workers take into these offices their existing attitudes towards work and, if anything, open-plan offices assist in cultivating dissent by convincing all concerned that they are small interchangeable cogs. It would take somebody with extreme optimism to argue that open-plan offices provide a suitable environment for all workers to gain fulfilment in their work.

Conclusion

The ideas of alienation and fulfilment provide people with some useful tools to evaluate the work they do. Rather than see these as static descriptions of distinct attitudes towards work, far more can be gained by viewing these ideas as existing along a continuum. It is quite possible that workers will fluctuate and change their positions on this continuum over time and within their careers, but seeing alienation and fulfilment as evaluative tools could allow them to set their priorities to measure their work against. In so doing, it might be possible for people to make clearer decisions about the work they do. We have seen the corrosive effects of alienation and could attribute these to the ethos of the capitalist system. Taking a hard line on this, it could be argued that alienation is a natural state under capitalism and that fulfilment at work is no more than a utopian promise, which could only be attained under a nonexploitative economic system. It should be evident, however, that many people seek fulfilment at work and will attempt as best they can to redesign their jobs to suit their needs. It will not always be the case that people will pursue greater economic power, but they might instead be motivated by the search for autonomy, creativity or sound relationships with work colleagues. Those who find themselves in an alienated state might have limited opportunities for fulfilment at work, but attempting to improve their working lives must surely begin with identifying their own priorities, aspirations and attitudes. Only then can they start to make constructive decisions about their own career development. We have noted in this chapter numerous barriers to fulfilment at work. In addition to the ethos of capitalism, we have seen how insecurity, a poor work–life balance, lack of opportunities and the working environment can all have a detrimental effect upon the way people view their work. We need to be aware, however, that workers are also located within hierarchies at work and that these power relations will also have an impact upon workers. We move on to consider these factors in the next chapter.

Questions to consider

1. What criteria would you use to assess the extent of your alienation or fulfilment in work?
2. To what extent is fulfilment in work important to you?
3. In what ways do you feel you are influenced by your working environment?

A guide to reading

The theoretical foundation for the issues of alienation and fulfilment is to be found in the works of Marx (1844) and Marx and Engels (1845) and in some of the most recent works by Bauman (2000 and 2005). For a management perspective, Richard Branson (2008) and Common Purpose (2004 and 2004a) are good places to start. The unions have also contributed to this debate. See in particular, the National Union of Teachers (2001), TUC (2010a and 2010b) and Unite (2010). There are also some useful articles in the quality press dealing with alienation, fulfilment and the working environment. These include Arnold (2009), Cartwright (2007) and Monaghan (2009) in *The Times*. Rushton (2013) appears in *The Telegraph*, whilst Bell (2005), Grigg (2008), Laurance (2008) and Paxman (2014) appeared in *The Guardian*. Finally, Susan Cain's quirky book, *Quiet* (2012), is full of insight on the importance of silence and the impact of the working environment.

References

Arnold, G. (2009) 'Stressful, underpaid, and it's downright dangerous', *The Times*, 8 May 2009, p. 2–3.

Atkins, J., Carter, D. and Nichol, M. (2002) *Reducing teachers' workload – a way forward*, National Union of Teachers and Association of Teachers and Lecturers. [online] Available from: http://www.teachers.org.uk/node/1094 [last accessed 17 July 2014].

Bauman, Z. (2000) *Liquid Modernity*, Polity: Cambridge.

Bauman, Z. (2005) *Work, Consumerism and the New Poor*, Open University Press: New York.

Bell, A. (2005) *Society life: Social work: Case study: Working in child protection is a family affair*, The Guardian, 28 September 2005, p. 2.

Branson, R. (2008) *Business Stripped Bare*, Virgin Books: London.

Cain, S. (2012) *Quiet*, Penguin: London.

Caplan, J. (2003) 'Police cynicism: Police survival tool?' *The Police Journal*, 76(4), pp. 1–6.

Cartwright, R. (2007) 'Social workers need support', *The Times*, 4 December 2007, p. 16.

Coats, D. and Lekhi, R. (2008) *Good work: Job quality in a changing economy*, The Work Foundation, http://theworkfoundation.com/Assets/Docs/good_work_final3.pdf (last accessed 17 July 2014).

Coats, D. and Max, C. (2005) *Healthy work: Productive workplaces*, The Work Foundation, The London Health Commission, http://www.theworkfoundation.com/assets/docs/publications/77_Healthy%20Work.pdf (last accessed 17 June 2014).

Commission on the Social Determinants of Health (2008), *Closing the gap in a generation*, http://whqlibdoc.who.int/publications/2008/9789241563703_eng_contents.pdf?ua=1 (last accessed, 17 July 2014).

Common Purpose (2004a) *Time for a change? A research report into the professional fulfillment experienced by tomorrow's leaders*, The Common Purpose Charitable Trust, http://www.commonpurpose.org.uk/resources/research.aspx (last accessed 17 July 2014).

Common Purpose (2004b) *Searching for something: Exploring the career traps and ambitions of young people*, The Common Purpose Charitable Trust, http://www.commonpurpose.org.uk/resources/research/release7.aspx (last accessed 17 July 2014).

de Botton, A. (2009) *The Pleasures and Sorrows of Work*, Hamish Hamilton: London.

Greenberg, E.S. and Grunberg, L. (2003) *The changing American workplace and the sense of mastery: assessing the impact of downsizing, job redesign and teaming*, University of Colorado, http://www.colorado.edu/IBS/pubs/pec/pec2003–0006.pdf (last accessed 17 July 2014).

Grigg, P. (2008) 'Passion in the workplace', *The Guardian*, 16 July 2008, http://www.guardian.co.uk/society/2008/jul/16/publicsectorcareers.youngpeople (last accessed 17 July 2014).

Grigg, P. and Lacey, J. (2008) 'Demanding good business'. In Keck, S. and Buonfino, A. (eds.) *The Future Face of Enterprise*, pp. 89–98, Demos, http://www.demos.co.uk/files/Demos_FutureFaceEnterprise_web.pdf (last accessed 17 July 2014).

Hodson, R. (2001) *Dignity at Work*, Cambridge University Press: Cambridge.

Hull, D. and Read, V. (2003) *Simply the best: Workplaces in Australia*, University of Sydney, http://www.business.vic.gov.au/busvicwr/_assets/main/lib60081/simply%20the%20best%20-%20workplaces%20in%20australia.pdf (last accessed 10 June 2010).

Illingworth, J. (2007) *Crazy about work*, Nottingham City Association of the National Union of Teachers [online] Available from: http://www.teachers.org.uk/node/5053 (last accessed 17 July 2014).

Jones, A. (2003) *About time for change*, The Work Foundation, http://www.theworkfoundation.com/assets/docs/publications/177_About%20time%20for%20change.pdf (last accessed 17 July 2014).

Laurance, J. (2008) 'Social workers need more support, too', *The Guardian*, 13 November 2008, p. 12.

Marx, K. (1844) *Economic and Philosophical Manuscripts of 1844*. Moscow: Progress Publishers (1959 edition).

Marx, K and Engels, F. (1845) *The German Ideology*, Lawrence and Wishart: London (1969 edition).

Mazza, C. (2008) 'Within these walls: The effects of environment on social work practice in prisons', *Practice: Social Work in Action*, Volume 20, Issue 4, pp. 251–264.

Molloy, A. (2013) 'Workplace: How to survive working in an open-plan office', *The Guardian*, 28 October 2013, p. 2.

Monaghan, G. (2009) 'The madness of open-plan offices', *The Sunday Times*, 8 February 2009, business section, p. 15.

Muirhead, R. (2004) 'Is your job just work?', *Harvard Business School*, 15 November 2004 (interviewed by M. Stark), http://hbswk.hbs.edu/archive/4487.html (last accessed 17 July 2014).

National Union of Teachers (2001) *Who's leaving? And why? Teachers' reasons for leaving the profession*, NUT. [online] Available from: http://www.teachers.org.uk/files/active/0/researchLeaversEE.pdf (Last accessed on 17 July 2014).

Oswald, A. (2002) *Are you happy at work? Job satisfaction and work-life balance in the US and Europe*, Warwick WBS Event, 5 November, Warwick Hotel, New York, http://www2.warwick.ac.uk/fac/soc/economics/staff/faculty/oswald/finalnywarwickwbseventpapernov2002.pdf (last accessed 17 July 2014).

Paxman, J. (2014) 'If I were king for a day I would banish open-plan offices', *The Guardian*, 13 September 2014, p. 39.

Reijula, J., Grohn, M., Muller, K. and Reijula, K., (2011) 'Human well-being and flowing work in an intelligent working environment', *Intelligent Buildings International*, Volume 3, Issue 4, pp. 223–237.

Rothi, D., Leavey, G. and Loewenthal, K. (2010) *Teachers' mental health: A study exploring the experiences of teachers with work-related stress and mental health problems*, NASWUT. [online] Available from: http://www.thedigitalpublisher.co.uk/mhealthreport2010 (last accessed 17 July 2014).

Rushton, K. (2013) 'New technology, invasions of privacy and the politics of the open plan office', *The Daily Telegraph*, 20 September 2013, business section, p. 2.

Svendsen, L. (2008) *Work*, Acumen: Durham.

TUC (2010a) *Teachers and lawyers most likely to work 'extreme' unpaid overtime*, Press release [online] issued 26 February 2010. Available from: http://www.tuc.org.uk/work_life/tuc-17614-f0.cfm (last accessed on 17 July 2014).

TUC (2010b) *In sickness and in health? Good work – and how to achieve it*, Trades Union Congress [online] Available from: http://www.tuc.org.uk/extras/goodwork.pdf (last accessed on 18 June 2010).

Unite (2010) '90% of charity workers feel under pressure as funding crisis mounts', Press release [online] issued 4 March 2010. Available from: http://www.epolitix.com/stakeholder-websites/press-releases/press-release-details/newsarticle/90-of-charity-workers-feel-under-pressure-as-funding-crisis-mounts///sites/unite-amicus-section/ (Last accessed on 18 June 2012).

Vischer, J. (2011) 'Towards an environmental psychology of workspace: How people are affected by environments for work', *Architectural Science Review*, Volume 51, Issue 2, pp. 97–108.

Watson, T. (2012) *Sociology, Work and Organisation*, Routledge: Oxon.

Work Foundation (2008) *Factsheet*, The Work Foundation, http://www.theworkfoundation.com/difference/e4wlb/factsheet.aspx (last accessed 17 July 2014).

chapter 4

Power, Control and Uncertainty at Work

The exercise of power and control at work can have a significant influence on the way people view their jobs and careers. We saw in the previous chapter on alienation and fulfilment that many people crave autonomy and respect at work and that inflexible approaches to management can have a damaging effect upon the way work is viewed. In order to analyse the impact of work upon people, we need to look beyond the individual and place workers within a social context. This chapter is going to focus upon the way that power and control influence the relationships between workers and how uncertainty at work serves the interests of employers. A distinction is made between power and control, though they are clearly closely related. The term power is used herein to refer to the ability to influence outcomes. This is a broad term which includes a range of associated concepts, including control. The term control is used in a narrower way and refers to the ability to circumvent conflict and create a compliant culture. Power and control are tools that can be used by management to secure their desired outcomes. We will see in chapter 5 how attempts to use these tools are not always successful, but for now the emphasis is upon identifying some of the distinctive features of power and control, how they operate in a variety of sectors and how the creation of uncertainty at work can undermine the confidence and self-esteem of workers.

Power

When we look at power, it is important that we take into account some of the ways in which power works on individuals. Power can be seen as the ability to control or influence (see Birch, 1993). It does not have to be active to exist. Some forms of power are latent. Consider, for example, the power of youth. This power builds up over time. It manifests itself in youth culture. It erupts sometimes and will eventually set the social and political agenda for the next generation. The exercise of power is often concerned with securing the compliance of others, though the methods for doing so vary considerably. Power can therefore include a range of kindred concepts, each of which provides a different way to gain the compliance of others. Lukes (2005) argues that power can operate through influence, coercion, force and manipulation. Whilst influence can be exerted without making any threats, coercion will often involve threatening to deprive somebody of something and force often relies upon depriving somebody of the choice of whether to comply. Where somebody is not aware of being influenced, we talk about manipulation. Whether power is viewed as a positive or negative force will ultimately depend upon one's politics. Viewed in an authoritarian light, power can be seen as a useful instrument to establish order, especially when this power is concentrated in the hands of the talented minority. From a more libertarian perspective, however, the unrestrained use of power poses a definite threat to civil rights and must therefore be tempered. When applied to the world of work, it is important to take note not only of the existence of power but also the mechanisms by which control is exerted. These associated concepts will allow us to view the worker within a network of power relations rather than as the holder of power or the one subjected to power.

Power and work

The success of management in securing the compliance and cooperation of workers will depend to a large extent upon the existing attitudes of workers towards their jobs. Those workers who have a relatively instrumental approach to work will tend to see work as a means to an end and will place far higher value upon their activities outside of work. Management will usually gain more from those who seek to position themselves within the hierarchy at work. These workers frequently ignore hard and fast distinctions between work and leisure and show they are willing to sacrifice some of the latter to enhance their position and even their sense of fulfilment by working towards nurturing or developing the organisation for which they work. We should bear in mind, however, that workers often work as part of a team. It is sometimes the case that workers will resist doing what is required by employers so as not to threaten the links they have with their colleagues. Cultures of resistance can develop within these clusters of workers (see Glover and Noon, 2005). The successful implementation of power relies not only upon the skills of those who wield power but also the cooperation of those who have less power.

The culture of fear

One way of seeking to exert power is through the cultivation of a culture of fear. This is where management leaves workers insecure and eager to please. Some managers choose to fluctuate in the way they deal with people and alternate between anger and friendliness on the grounds that it keeps the workers on their toes. According to Templar (2003), this can generate fear and uncertainty but rarely respect. Coercive supervision is often used to secure the compliance of workers performing low-level tasks. This in turn can lead to higher levels of conflict between the workers and management. Rather than respond by finding ways to build trust between management and workers, organisations will resort to monitoring the performance of their workers (see Watson, 2003 and 2012). This approach to management and use of power does not necessarily produce an effective workforce, nor does it guarantee to bring out the best in people. Some employers would much prefer to find a way to empower their workers in the hope of liberating their creativity and sense of responsibility in the work they do. This is the approach that Richard Branson claims works well at Virgin (see Branson, 2008). It should be evident that the success or otherwise of creating a culture of fear will depend upon the type of work being carried out. It is quite possibly the case that this culture can reap dividends for management where the workers are expected to perform mundane tasks. A culture of fear, however, can also exert unnecessary pressure upon workers and reduce their creativity and productivity. The emotions generated by a culture of fear need to be processed by workers and this in itself is enough to cut into their dedication and commitment at work.

Power and the problems of poor management in teaching

When entering a profession, workers will have expectations of their management. These could be based upon the advice and information they receive about their particular employer or from the way workers view their own skills. A number of studies (see National Union of Teachers, 2001; Owen, Broadhurst and Keats, 2009) have looked into the expectations and experiences of newly qualified teachers and have showed the damage inflicted on workers by poor management and lack of support. Newly qualified teachers have complained that they are often deprived of clear guidance on school policy and admit that they would change schools to free themselves from poor management and lack of clarity in the structure of their careers. For more experienced staff, opportunities for promotion can be particularly important and schools can lose good staff because they fail to provide their staff with suitable opportunities for professional development (see Owen et al., 2009). According to the National Union of Teachers (2001), newly qualified teachers are frequently shocked by the pressure of work and the lack of support from senior colleagues and management. Unsupported and disheartened, many will choose to leave the profession and train for a less stressful career. These studies looking into the experiences of teachers are important in showing how the indifference of senior colleagues and management can undermine the confidence of newly qualified teachers and make them unable to function well in their work. Power can be exercised by depriving people of sufficient guidance and thereby leaving them uncertain about how to find their feet and to progress at work.

The illusion of social mobility

Progression through the social hierarchy cannot be guaranteed through attaining proficiency at work but will also rely upon a variety of social factors. According to Bourdieu (1986), the possession of 'cultural capital' is particularly important in influencing the opportunities open to people. This cultural capital stems not only from what individuals accumulate from their education but also from the deep-seated influence of family backgrounds. Social mobility is far from widespread. It has been argued that '. . . young people who enter the workforce today are less likely to move up in the social hierarchy than their parents were' (Svendsen, 2008, p. 54). Whilst there are notable exceptions to the rule, very few people will ever make the transition from rags to riches. Alain de Botton (2009), for example, claims that '. . . the likelihood of reaching the pinnacle of capitalist society today is only marginally better than were the chances of being accepted into the French nobility four centuries ago, though at least an aristocratic age was franker, and therefore kinder, about the odds' (de Botton, 2009, p. 278). Those who desire to progress in this way will also tend to be in the minority. Moving through an occupational hierarchy has a price. The fulfilment and autonomy craved by many workers is not necessarily more prevalent in the higher echelons of organisations. Indeed, as workers rise through a hierarchy, they will often have to take on more responsibilities and can become more isolated from fellow workers. Students have found that it is important to understand how hierarchies operate at work and to adapt as best they can (see box 4a).

We have seen that power is a tool used in the context of instability at work. Managers are in a position to galvanise the energies of their team by taking into account what people want from their work. Whilst some managers will no doubt seek to provide their team with what they want or at least need, others will look to take advantage of the career aspirations of their juniors to further their own agendas. Using the example of newly qualified teachers, we have noted how when people take on a new job they enter into an existing network of power. Part of their socialisation process involves coming to grips with the exercise of power and finding their own place in the network of power relations. It is important to recognise the dynamics of power and to see that the exercise of power has consequences and will often generate resistance (this is covered in more detail in chapter 5). If power is viewed as the possession of management, however, we will miss some of the subtle ways in which power is exerted. More can be gained by looking at the mechanisms used in control.

Control

Control can be exerted in a way that disguises the very existence of power. Lukes (2005) warned against placing too much emphasis upon observable conflict because it failed to give credence to the ways in which power is also exerted by influencing our preferences. Indeed, Lukes asks '. . . is it not the supreme exercise of power to get another or others to have the desires you want them to have – that is, to secure their compliance by controlling their thoughts and desires?' (Lukes, 2005, p. 27). Rather than concentrate upon observable conflict, Lukes was interested in asking why conflict is not more widespread, and he firmly believed that it is the '. . . most effective and insidious use of power to prevent such conflict from arising in the first place' (Lukes, 2005, p. 27). He acknowledged that this view of power was influenced by Marxist and feminist writings, as both reflect upon '. . . the capacity to secure compliance to domination through the shaping of beliefs and desires, by imposing internal constraints under historically changing circumstances' (Lukes, 2005, p. 144). Control, defined in this way, is exercised when those who are controlled buy into particular ideas or behaviours which make it easier for their behaviour to be controlled and for conflict and resistance to be minimised. Although those who seek to control will not always be successful, the attempt to do so will involve a certain approach to power which places less emphasis on force and more upon securing compliance.

Management and the illusion of control

Although managers might like to give the impression that they are in control, it is apparent that not all managers are comfortable with their role and have to find ways to conceptualise and project their role to those they manage. Watson (2012) draws attention to reluctant managers, who find they are unable to disengage from work but need to maintain their professional commitment. He claims that managers, especially in the middle tier, will often make use of particular discourses surrounding professional identity in order to give a foundation or anchor to their role in work and to the way they see themselves. Part of this might include a reluctance to use the term manager, in the belief that it has negative connotations because of its association with bureaucracy, and make use of such terms as project leader instead. Watson claims that managers sometimes project enthusiasm at work or latch on to fads and fashions in the hope of concealing their inner fears and insecurities. It should be noted that by embracing the new and by attempting to innovate, managers might also try to explain away problems that occur at work by claiming that such teething problems are bound to occur and that these are justified in the name of progress. Watson's work on the reluctant manager illustrates that control by management is contingent upon projecting certain messages and that the maintenance of control is by no means guaranteed. It could be argued, indeed, that creating the illusion of control is one of the key functions of a manager.

Control through bureaucracy in social work and the public sector

Although bureaucracy could be seen as a way to establish a set of rules and procedures for an organisation, it can also be seen as a mechanism through which workers are controlled by placing limits on their autonomy and by creating a restrictive culture at work. In a study based upon 40 interviews with social workers in Britain, Jones (2001) noted how social workers had become disheartened with their work because an increasing amount of time was being spent on bureaucratic tasks, filling in forms and taking part in audits. Although these workers remained committed to the welfare of their clients, they invariably felt that their profession was being damaged by a shift towards a new managerial culture based upon rigid adherence to procedures and protocols. Kirkpatrick (2006) noted how social workers were monitored continually and how this diminished their autonomy and their satisfaction at work. Kirkpatrick argued that social workers were once attracted to the profession in the belief that it was a noble vocation but that the audit culture and constant monitoring had led to the intensification of work and increased work-related stress. Stress also mounts because of the development of a blame culture. Social workers and civil servants in particular have found this has had a harmful effect upon their experience of work (see Rose, 2006). Commenting upon his experience of the private and public sectors, Luke Johnson, the former chair of Channel 4 in the UK, claimed that whilst the private sector encourages people to take risks, the public sector tends to make workers timid and afraid to take responsibility. Public sector workers, in his experience, tend to push decisions onto their line managers rather than take responsibility themselves. A work culture dominated by conformity and hierarchy is in this way created because of a fear of failure (Johnson, 2006). Bureaucracy can thus be used to instil fear in workers and to protect a hierarchy. Although workers might be critical of those in more senior positions, the price of failure and the recognition that hierarchies are entrenched and surrounded by bureaucratic procedures will often be enough to dissuade workers from pushing for promotion.

Bullying and control

Workers can also be controlled through bullying. This does not need to be through physical intimidation but can be exerted in more devious ways. According to the TUC (2010), workers are often bullied by management through depriving them of opportunities for advancement, being given tasks to do beneath their abilities, setting unrealistic deadlines and through excluding workers from particular activities. When this is allowed to continue, workers will often produce poorer quality work, become more stressed, less productive and generally less settled. According to the arbitration service ACAS (2008), workers are far more happy and productive where they are involved in the decision-making process and given support by their managers, though this does not mean that they will have freedom to determine when and how they work. Control by bullying is not only confined to those subject to bullying. Witnessing a culture of bullying might be enough to clip the wings of other workers and make them act in a way to divert attention away from themselves in the hope of becoming less likely to be bullied.

Foucault and surveillance culture

One of the key ways to exert control is through the use of surveillance. Michel Foucault refers to this as a form of disciplinary power, which he explains by drawing attention to the idea of a panoptican in his book *Discipline and Punish* (Foucault, 1977). The panoptican consisted in a building designed to observe prisoners. Instead of locking these prisoners away in a dark dungeon, the panoptican relies upon exposing prisoners to light. The building would be divided into cells and built around a central tower where an observer sits and observes. The prisoners would be separated from one another but could always be subject to surveillance from an observer. In order to work effectively, the prisoners would not know when they were being observed because the windows of the observation tower would be shuttered. Indeed, the prisoners would not even know if they were ever observed. This design for a prison was thought useful for breaking down any sense of unity amongst prisoners and encouraging them to behave as if they were being observed. It is thought that over time, people start to censor their own behaviour (see Foucault, 1977, pp. 200–207; Merquior, 1991, p. 91). This provides a way to exert control by enlisting the support of the observed.

Foucault and the automatic exercise of power

Foucault believes that the panoptican provides a way for power to function automatically and that it creates a power relationship independent of those exercising power. He claimed that a person who knows that he or she might be observed '. . . assumes responsibility for the constraints of power' (Foucault 1977, p. 201). In this way, a person internalises power and becomes '. . . the principle of his own subjection' (Foucault, 1977, pp. 201–202). Power in the panoptican operates regardless of the intentions of the observer. It provides a way to affect people's behaviour and to impose discipline in a subtle way. This method, according to Foucault, is effective because it can be applied to the majority by relatively few people and because it provides the user with power over the minds of others. He thought the panoptican could be used whenever it was important to alter the behaviour of those held captive in some way or another. In his view, it could be used to reform prisoners, instruct children, treat psychiatric patients and control workers and even increase their productivity. Foucault is by no means advocating its use. He simply points out that disciplinary power has a variety of applications and is effective.

Adaptations of Foucault on disciplinary power and work

Foucault's views on power can be seen in the writings of a number of commentators on the sociology of work. According to Deetz (2000), corporate identity rests upon the illusion of freedom and the belief that the working environment can operate without conflict (Deetz, 2000, p. 147). Power is said to be dispersed unevenly in modern corporations and '. . . spreads out through lines of conformity, commonsense observations and determinations of propriety' (Deetz, 2000, p. 156). He claimed that power can operate without direct managerial intervention and that managers only need to intervene when power relations break down. In his view, there is a culture of self-surveillance, especially in managerial levels of organisations, because '. . . the employee can never tell who might use what against him or her or when a statement will come back to cause one's own demise' (Deetz, 2000, p. 158). This adaptation of Foucault shows how disciplinary power is embedded within modern corporations and allows these to run by creating a culture of self-surveillance in which workers censor their own behaviour.

Foucault's influence can also be seen in the work of Keith Grint (see Grint, 1998), who draws a distinction between modernist and postmodernist views of work. He claims that modernists believe that modern corporations provide a rational way to manage people by helping to create stability and certainty in the workplace. Postmodernists, on the other hand, are thought to believe that corporations provide mechanisms to control workers, undermine freedom and are thus '. . . the results of reactive processes, attempts to delimit the disaggregating reality of everyday existence' (Grint, 1998, p. 139). Drawing directly from Foucault, he notes how surveillance techniques allow corporations to observe their workers and control their lives. Grint thus illustrates how the modernist faith in corporations as rational and benevolent merely disguises their oppressive nature and the way they exert control over workers.

The impact of surveillance on workers

Making use of surveillance techniques at work could be seen as a way to monitor workers and improve productivity. By keeping workers under observation, managers might think this will ensure that workers work consistently hard and, in true Foucauldian fashion, censor their own behaviour.

The effectiveness of surveillance techniques, however, is far from proven. Wylie (2005) claims that the use of surveillance to monitor employees undermines trust in the workplace. This applies notoriously in call centres where managers are able to keep track of workers throughout the day. Work in call centres can be monitored closely because management can listen to calls, observe workers and evaluate their work with relative ease. Lee and Kleiner (2003) note by the end of the 20th century, over two thirds of companies in the United States made use of some form of electronic surveillance of their workers. Whilst employers have argued that the use of surveillance techniques helps to increase the productivity of workers and assists in maintaining levels of quality, workers claim that it increases levels of stress and undermines their trust and loyalty towards their employer. Indeed, the existence of surveillance techniques signals to workers that they are not trusted by their employers, and they are thus less likely to feel motivated in the work they do. Students have noted how surveillance has had a significant impact upon their experience of work (see box 4b).

4b: Students on disciplinary power and surveillance

Beth recalled that she started to feel alienated because of being subject to constant surveillance, which destroyed any pleasure she could gain from work and made her feel disengaged from the work she did (Beth). Laura talked about feeling the constant presence of managers as they observed their staff through the use of CCTV. She was aware that this potential presence influenced the way she interacted with customers and acknowledged that it '. . . made me lose trust and respect for the managers as I felt that they were only monitoring what we did wrong rather than rewarding us for doing something right' (Laura). Students have experienced the sensation of constant surveillance of their work within call centres, though this is not always seen in a negative light. Through receiving real-time information on her work in a call centre, Naomi said that it allowed her to '. . . track myself constantly to see how my performance is throughout the day' (Naomi). Chris pointed out that his work in a call centre was open to surveillance from management and that this ensured that correct procedures were followed. He did, however, recognise that this made him censor his own behaviour (Chris). These comments show that surveillance can be viewed in a positive and negative way, depending upon whether the students regarded the surveillance as intrusive or as an aid for them to use in pacing their work and developing the skills they need to work effectively.

By focusing upon the way that control is exerted at work, it is possible to see some of the illusions created in the interest of securing compliance. Instability at work, the pressure of corporate agendas and the apparent thirst for innovation can be used by management to destabilise workers and to explain away problems by claiming they result from a temporary set of circumstances. Management might also seek to exert control through instituting audits, increasing observation of workers, encouraging fear of failure and through limiting opportunities for particular people. But managers also need to ensure that they are insulated from too much criticism. One way of doing this is through encouraging workers to censor their own behaviour by using surveillance technology. Examples from social work, the public sector and call centres have been used to illustrate these mechanisms of control. We need to bear in mind, however, that these are merely frameworks that can be used if management so wishes. There is no reason to believe that these frameworks are applied in a uniform manner across all groups of workers. Broader social inequalities will also have a part to play. As we move on in this analysis, it is important to take a look at some of the vulnerable sections of the workforce who endure uncertainty at work as a result of working on poor contracts.

Uncertainty at work

If workers are unable to find their feet at work or have the stability they crave, then work can become a source of anxiety. Bauman (2000) notes how work has become increasingly uncertain as people are offered short-term contracts and limited career opportunities. He claims that workers tend to regard their place of employment as a temporary resting place rather than as something they can rely upon in the long term. Workers are thought to see themselves as disposable and therefore avoid attaching any great significance to their work or place great value upon developing stable relationships with their colleagues. Bauman believes that rather than seeking to enhance the general good of their place of employment, it makes more sense for workers to think in terms of their own private interests and their own immediate prospects. Instead of fighting for their rights within organisations, it would appear that workers are more likely to change jobs when the organisation fails to deliver a satisfying work experience (see Bauman, 2000). Bauman's analysis gives the impression that uncertainty and instability at work are systemic problems stemming from the dominant characteristics of the age. He notes that the stability of identity and of roles have been undermined by the pressures of the globalised economy and by the apparent preference for rapid change and that this has created a climate within which uncertainty and instability are accepted. We will now look at some of the ways uncertainty manifests itself at work.

The impact of temporary work

Although people in temporary work can often feel good about their work in the short term, levels of job satisfaction can drop sharply for those workers trapped in short-term contracts. Temporary workers might feel less committed to their jobs and find it more difficult to attribute meaning to their work. Having to fill in wherever necessary prevents temporary workers from developing expertise in their field and from gaining the specialist knowledge often deemed essential for a permanent post (see Svendsen, 2008). Management will often use temporary contracts to vet people. Graaf-Zijl, Berg and Heyma (2011) claimed that temporary work can benefit workers by providing them with opportunities to try new occupations and determine to what extent they feel comfortable in that work environment. They also point out that that some employers might be reluctant to offer full-time contracts to particular groups in society, especially new arrivals from different cultures, but that temporary contracts provide employers with time to assess the suitability of these workers to their organisation. Unions can sometimes find themselves in a difficult position when considering how to approach workers on temporary contracts. According to Pulignano and Doerflinger (2013), trade unions in Belgium and Germany often find that, despite their declared opposition to the principle of workers being offered temporary work, they have to accept the use of temporary agency staff in order to relieve the pressure of work on workers with permanent contracts. Unions have also been instrumental in promoting the rights of temporary agency staff and pushing for the staff to be placed on permanent contracts. It is clear, however, that failure of employers to provide workers with stability sends out a strong signal that whilst some workers are essential to their operation, others are disposable and worthy of less consideration.

Zero-hours contracts

Under a system of zero-hours contracts, workers are not guaranteed stable work and will find that the amount they work each week or month will often vary greatly. These contracts are used across many sectors of employment and account for approximately 20% of workers in hospitality, 7% in retail and 60% in care work (Butler and Neville, 2013). Political parties in Britain have been slow to respond to the problem of zero-hours contracts. Although generally in favour of a deregulated labour market, the Conservative Party has often tried to avoid being pulled into defending the principles of zero-hour contracts (see Hardman, 2013). At the Conservative Party conference in 2014, however, David Cameron (see Cameron, 2014) condemned those employers who seek to prevent their workers working for a range of employers. In his view, this was inconsistent with a flexible and free labour market. For the Labour Party (2015), zero-hours contracts place an unnecessary strain upon workers and their families. The Labour Party pledges to extend the rights of workers on zero-hours contracts by allowing them to work for multiple employers, having the right to compensation for work cancelled at short notice and the right to a permanent contract if they have worked for the same employer consistently.

There are understandable differences between the way that employers and unions view zero-hours contracts. Percival (2014) argues the case for zero-hours contracts from the employers' perspective. He claims that zero-hours contracts are valued because they are flexible, they protect jobs and they allow employers to avoid making redundancies during downturns in the economy. In his view, zero-hours contracts help to keep businesses in Britain competitive and allow employers to respond rapidly to fluctuating demands for their goods and services. He is convinced, moreover, that these contracts also benefit workers by providing them with the freedom to determine when they work. This is deemed particularly important for women with family commitments, people nearing the end of their working lives and students needing to combine paid work with their studies. According to the trade union Unite (2013), zero-hours contracts hit young people and ethnic minorities in particular and benefit the employers far more than the workers. These types of contracts allow employers to reduce their expenditure on their workers and to dictate to workers when they can and cannot work. Zero-hours contracts are thought to increase the insecurity of workers and undermine the stability of the economy.

The use of temporary contracts and zero-hours contracts can be viewed as another way for employers to exert control over workers. The benefits for employers are clear because these contracts allow employers to avoid making a financial commitment to workers by taking them on when needed and picking and choosing the workers they want to employ. Although some workers will no doubt value the flexibility afforded by temporary and zero-hours contracts, these have clearly been devised by employers in their own interest. Whilst declaring opposition to zero-hours and temporary contracts, the Labour Party and unions are cautious in their policies so as to not alienate businesses and to provide employers with the flexibility to hire workers to reduce the pressure upon workers with full-time contracts. By creating uncertainty at work, short-term and zero-hours contracts can create greater levels of anxiety for significant sections of the working population.

Conclusion

The concepts of power and control can be used to understand the relationships between workers and the choices they make in their working lives. The form of power and control used will vary depending upon the sector of employment, the characteristics of the workforce and the attitudes of management. The culture created at work relies not only upon the input of management but also the ways in which workers adapt. Workers will have to decide where they want to be in a hierarchy. They will choose whether to pursue power or to find a level more suited to their current skills and dispositions. Senior management will no doubt look for those who can assist them in the development of their business model, whilst creating at least some obstacles to progression so as to preserve their own power base. Power and control will influence not only the relationship between management and employees but also the way workers relate to each other. Workers may choose to form friendships and associations at work based upon shared attitudes towards the mechanisms of power and control used. By stating their attitudes towards their employers, workers display their own values and illustrate to their fellow workers where their loyalties lie. The ability to read the culture of a workplace can help workers to navigate their way through work and make some informed decisions about how far they wish to progress. Having some understanding of power and control should provide workers with insight into the ways that managers attempt to make use of the human resources at their disposal. For some workers, this will mean being deprived of stability in their employment, which in turn can deprive them of power and influence with their employers and with colleagues on more stable contracts. As we will see in the next chapter, workers have had to develop a variety of ways to resist the power of management.

Questions to consider

1. To what extent is it important to understand hierarchies at work?
2. In what ways can the use of surveillance in workplaces enhance the quality of service provided?
3. What mechanisms are used by management to place limits on the power of workers?

A guide to reading

The theoretical foundations power, control and uncertainty can be found in Luke's views on the importance of circumventing conflict (2005), Bourdieu's writings on cultural capital (1986), Foucault's work on disciplinary power (1977) and Bauman's observations on the impact of short-term contracts (2000). For general works on power and control in work see Glover and Noon (2005), Watson (2012), de Botton (2009) and Svendsen (2008). Grint (1998), Deetz (2000) and Wylie (2005) deal with disciplinary power and work. For a managerial perspective, see Branson (2008) and Percival (2014). National Union of Teachers (2001), TUC (2010) and Unite (2013) express the union perspective.

References

ACAS (2008) *Health, work and wellbeing*, ACAS, [online] Available from: http://www. acas.org.uk/index.aspx?articleid=693 (last accessed 23 July 2010).

Bauman, Z. (2000) *Liquid Modernity*, Polity: Cambridge.

Birch, A. H. (1993) *The Concepts and Theories of Modern Democracy*, Routledge: London.

Bourdieu, P. (1986) 'The forms of capital'. In J.E. Richardson (ed) (1986) *Handbook of Theory of Research for the Sociology of Education*, Greenwood Press: New York, pp. 241–258.

Branson, R. (2008) *Business Stripped Bare*, Virgin Books: London.

Butler, D. and Neville, S. (2013) 'Hovis staff to start strike over zero hours contracts', *The Guardian*, 28 August 2013, p. 25.

Cameron, D. (2014) 'Speech to Conservative Party conference', http://press.conserv atives.com/post/98882674910/david-cameron-speech-to-conservative-party (last accessed 10 March 2015).

de Botton, A. (2009) *The Pleasures and Sorrows of Work*, Hamish Hamilton: London.

Deetz, S. (2000) 'Discipline'. In K. Grint (ed) (2000) *Work and Society: A Reader*, Polity: Cambridge, pp. 142–162.

Foucault, M. (1977) *Discipline and Punish*, Penguin: Harmondsworth.

Glover, L. and Noon, M. (2005) 'Shop-floor workers' responses to quality management initiatives: Broadening the disciplined worker thesis', *Work, Employment & Society*, Volume 25, Issue 4, pp. 760–776.

Graaf-Zijl, M., Berg, G. and Heyma, A. (2011) 'Steppingstones for the unemployed: the effect of temporary work on the duration until (regular) work', *Journal of Population Economics*, Volume 24, Issue 1, pp. 107–139.

Grint, K. (1998) *The Sociology of Work*, Polity Press: Cambridge.

Hardman, I. (2013) 'What do the Tories think about zero hours contracts? They don't seem very keen to tell us', *The Spectator*, 9 July 2013, http://blogs.spectator.co.uk/cof feehouse/2013/07/what-do-the-tories-think-about-zero-hours-contracts-they-dont-seem-very-keen-to-tell-us/ (last accessed 10 March 2015).

Johnson, L. (2006) 'Survival of the fittest favours the public sector', *The Sunday Telegraph*, 12 February 2006, p. 4.

Jones, C. (2001) 'Voices from the front line: State social worker and New Labour', *British Journal of Social Work*, Volume 31, pp. 547–562.

Kirkpatrick, I. (2006) 'Taking stock of the new managerialism in English social services', *New Professionalism in Social Work*, Volume 4, Issue 1, pp. 1–12.

Labour Party (2015) 'Job security: A labour government will end exploitative zero-hours contracts', http://www.labour.org.uk/issues/detail/zero-hours-contracts (last accessed 16 April 2015).

Lee, S. and Kleiner, B. (2003) 'Electronic surveillance in the workplace', *Management Research News*, Volume 26, pp. 72–81.

Lukes, S. (2005) *Power: A Radical View*, Palgrave: Basingstoke.

Merquior, J. G. (1991) *Foucault*, Fontana: Glasgow.

National Union of Teachers (2001) *Who's leaving? And why? Teachers' reasons for leaving the profession*, NUT, http://www.teachers.org.uk/files/active/0/researchLeaversEE. pdf (last accessed 17 July 2014).

Owen, K., Broadhurst, K. and Keats, G. (2009) *Sink or Swim? Learning Lessons from Newly Qualified and Recently Qualified Teachers: A Study Examining How Initial Teacher Training and In-School Support Prepares Teachers for Their Careers*, NASUWT: Birmingham.

Percival, M. (2014) 'Zero hours contracts: Encouraging flexibility that benefits employers and employees', CBI, http://www.cbi.org.uk/media/2628041/zero_hours_con tracts.pdf (last accessed March 2015).

Pulignano, V. and Doerflinger, N (2013) 'A head with two tales: Trade unions' influence on temporary agency work in Belgian and German workplaces', *The International Journal of Human Resource Management*, Volume 24, Issue 22, pp. 4149–4165.

Rose, D. (2006) 'Priory inundated with civil servants', *The Times*, 29 November 2006, p.29.

Svendsen, L (2008) *Work*, Acumen: Durham.

Templar, R. (2003) *The Rules of Work*, Pearson: Harlow.

TUC (2010) *Bullied at work? Don't suffer in silence*; TUC [online] Available from: http://www.tuc.org.uk/tuc/rights_bullyatwork.cfm [last accessed on 19 July 2010].

Unite (2013) Zero hours contracts brief, http://www.unitetheunion.org/uploaded/documents/001-Zero%20hours%20contracts%20brief-v211–12576.pdf (last accessed March 2015).

Watson, T. (2003) *Sociology, Work and Industry*, Routledge: London, 2003 (4th edition).

Watson, T (2012) *Sociology, Work and Organisation*, Routledge: Oxon.

Wylie, I. (2005) 'Work: Crisis of faith', *The Guardian*, 24 September 2005, p. 3.

chapter 5

Conflict, Resistance and Change Management

The exercise of power and attempts to control workers can give rise to conflict at work and to workers engaging in various forms of resistance. Although management might be keen to identify and strengthen common commitment to the needs of the employer, conflicts do develop. These could be interpersonal conflicts, stemming from different attitudes or approaches to work. Managers might be able to deal with these on a case-by-case basis, but conflicts can also arise because of deeply ingrained social divisions. These divisions, especially those based on class or gender, are rather less open to quick remedies. In order to see how conflict develops at work, we will take a look at the experiences of workers in different sectors and at how conflicts between different groups manifest themselves. Workers will often find ways to resist attempts to control their activities. Some of the different methods of resistance will be examined, including those that are overt and challenging and those that are covert and subtle. By no means are all forms of resistance designed to challenge the status quo. Indeed, it is often the case that workers are looking for ways to survive with their identity and dignity intact. We will also take a look at the implications of conflict and resistance for the ways in which change is managed. Rather than view resistance in a negative way, an attempt will be made to trace some of the reasons for resistance to change and to show how resistance can be useful in scrutinising proposals for change and in introducing changes to benefit workers as well as employers.

Conflict

Conflict is often rooted in differences in class position, gender, ethnicity and so on. Conflict can be overt and visible but it can also exist under the surface of an apparent consensus. According to Beck (2000), many of the key conflicts in society have become institutionalised and made to fit within a prescribed framework. This has occurred so as to protect society from open conflict and it is argued that the '. . . demonisation of social and political conflicts to their recognition within civilised procedures establishes a crucial yardstick for measuring the actual modernity of ostensibly modern societies' (Beck, 2000, p. 173). This is important, especially when we consider how conflict exists in the workplace. According to Watson (2003 and 2012), conflict at work can occur when there are differences between individuals over the outcomes they want and when individuals engage in destructive behaviour. He points out, however, that conflict is not necessarily bad and that it is important to view conflict in terms of the issues at stake. He identifies four key approaches to conflict at work, which he termed the free market, unitary, pluralist and radical approaches. The free market approach identifies tensions developing between workers and employers because both seek to maximise their own self-interests. This approach does not, however, condemn the free market, because the free market is thought to allow for an optimal balance between these interests. The unitary approach works on the assumption that there are common interests uniting people working in a particular organisation and that the role of the manager is to identify and promote these common interests. This approach to conflict at work regards opposition from workers as irrational and disloyal. The pluralist approach acknowledges that conflicts exist and looks for ways to compromise. Pluralists recognise the importance of entering into negotiations with workers and looking for common ground. Finally, the radical approach to conflict sees that systemic inequalities prevent compromises from being reached in the interest of all workers. According to this approach to conflict, inequalities in power mean that some groups will dominate others.

Building commitment

In an attempt to encourage common commitment to an employer, employers will sometimes try to gain the loyalty of workers by appealing to the importance of the brand. According to Fram and McCarthy (2003), companies can gain a great deal from spending resources on marketing their product to their employees. They argue that employees can become important champions of the products they produce and those employees who display a high level of brand loyalty are also more likely to feel fulfilled at work and be more supportive towards the priorities and strategies presented by management. Supermarkets like ASDA pride themselves on building a strong sense of team through encouraging informality between grades, regular consultation and through promoting share ownership amongst the workforce (see White, 2003). Some workers will express their loyalty to their employer by engaging in activities above and beyond those required by the organisation. This commitment often stems from the hope that the production of a commodity or the provision of a service can be improved through innovation and hard work (see Hodson, 2001). The more an employer can build loyalty to a product or service, the easier it becomes to manage conflict. Where there is a high commitment to the brand or to the ethos of a company, managers are able to appeal to values existing outside and above the individual worker. Under these circumstances, an argument could be made to encourage a sense of common sacrifice or even devotion to a cause. Managers might therefore ask workers to put aside their differences or brush aside minor grievances because their work is useful, important or fulfilling.

Dealing with conflicting interests

Conflict is part of the lifeblood of some sectors of employment. Those involved in politics will spend most of their time dealing with conflicts of one sort or another. This can be seen in the advice given by William Waldegrave (see Waldegrave, 2010) to Danny Alexander when he took on the role of chief secretary to the Treasury. Waldegrave, who had performed this role in John Major's government during the 1990s, told Alexander that his main role is to negotiate budgets with each minister and to inform the chancellor of the exchequer of these negotiations. He warned that the chief secretary must be able to judge when to fight and which battles can be won and claimed that '. . . if you outmanoeuvre a dim colleague too far, and cut his or her programme beyond what is reasonable, you will have to give it back later' (Waldegrave, 2010, p. 21). In his view, the chief secretary to the Treasury must be able to push ministers to identify their priorities for spending and be willing to cut provision across the board if ministers fail to identify what is important and what is not. Working at the cutting edge of politics, those who perform this role must clearly have the ability to handle conflict and to maintain focus on broader strategic objectives. Although power bases will develop within each department, the chief secretary to the Treasury is still able to call for sacrifice to the common good, which, in this case, is the strategic and monetary priority of the government.

Conflicts are sometimes deeply personal. In politics, these tend to attract far more attention in the media. Politics can, indeed, sometimes seem like a battle between individuals rather than an ideological war. Consider, for example, the conflict between Tony Blair and Gordon Brown. When Tony Blair (2010) wrote in his autobiography about the problems he encountered in his relationship with Gordon Brown, he recalled that Gordon Brown had become a force of resistance in the Blair government. Blair valued Brown's ability as chancellor of the exchequer. He also knew that he would have to stand down eventually and that Gordon Brown was his likely successor. He tried to use this as a bargaining chip in his relationship with Brown. It appears as if Gordon Brown was left in limbo for many years and it was not until Blair felt he had lost touch with his own party and with the British electorate that he agreed to go. As soon as he started to lose authority in his party, and no doubt learning a lesson from the fall of Margaret Thatcher in the early 1990s, Blair stood down as leader and thereby allowed room for Brown and his supporters to fill the vacuum.

Conflict can be alleviated to some extent when people recognise that each individual has something different to offer in the workplace. In many cases, workers have to find ways to cooperate with those who perform different functions and whose outlook on a particular workplace will be very different. Al Pacino, for example, noted that actors and directors have different perspectives on the films they create. Whilst directors will know how to structure a film, actors tend to know rather more about dialogue. He claimed that it was essential for directors and actors to find some common ground and that even the best conceived scripts can fall short of the mark if actors and directors are unable to agree on their approach to their work and on the tone and meaning of a film. He recalled that his work on *Bobby Deerfield* suffered because of the differences between his own interpretation and that of Sydney Pollack, the director. Pacino admitted that he did not really appreciate what Pollack was trying to achieve, and he admitted that '. . . we would have been better off had I listened to him more' (Pacino in Grobel (ed), 2006, p. 64). This shows how conflict can develop because individuals will have not only different levels of expertise but also different types of expertise. The same could be said about the different skills of frontline workers and those who work behind the scenes in teaching, social work and a range of professions. Frontline workers will develop their understanding of their work through interacting with their client group, whilst those who coordinate or administer this work will draw their knowledge and expertise from different sources and will no doubt be driven rather more by guidelines and protocols set from above.

Conflict and systemic inequalities

Some conflicts develop not because of the nature of the work but because of systemic inequalities. Watson (2003) claims that there are problems with the way that work is organised and that these can create instability in the system. Major problems occur because of inequality. Dominant groups may well promote certain values or goals but effectively exclude many from accessing these goals or achieving success. Watson notes that Western cultures place a high value on individual freedom but '. . . the great majority of people in their work experience find themselves under the control and domination of others to a degree which potentially clashes with cultural expectations' (Watson, 2003, p.216). The freedom and autonomy people might desire is thus curtailed in a work setting and this can be exacerbated because of differences in the economic and political power of different classes and genders.

Conflict and class

According to Marx and Engels (1848), class conflict in work is inescapable under capitalism, because employers will develop ways to exploit workers through investment in technology and because of their need to expand their share of the market due to the pressures of competition from other companies. Marx and Engels saw that employers will explore ways to cut costs and this will often result in attacking the standard of living of their workers. Under these conditions, they believed that workers will start to fight back through resistance to technology, through union activity and, finally, revolutionary activity. This fairly crude position on class conflict was developed in the *Manifesto of the Communist Party* and has remained an important feature of the Marxist approach. Whilst Marxists will seek to apply this to the politics of economic, social and political change, it can also serve as a foundation for understanding conflict at work. Rather than blame individual employers for exploiting workers and seeking to squeeze more from their workforce, the Marxist perspective can be used to show that employers are to a large extent following the rules and protocols of the capitalist system and are often struggling to survive in a hostile market. To the extent that this is the case, workers also need to find ways to defend themselves. This might be through negotiation with the employer, strike action or through broader political activity.

Conflict and gender

Inequalities between men and women are also evident in the workplace. Paul Ransome (1999) argues that we have a patriarchal economic system defined by patriarchal relations at home and at work and that there has been a shift from private patriarchy to public patriarchy through the subordination of women at work. He claims that jobs are gendered in a variety of ways, including the stipulation of either physical or psychological requirements for a job, the widespread preference of maintaining single-sex teams and because women often want to work shorter hours. He notes that part-time employment is dominated by women, and this can have serious consequences for their pensions, entitlement to leave, access to health benefits and to maternity pay. In his view, men often protect their positions by creating an exclusive club that creates barriers to the advancement of women colleagues.

The battles that women sometimes have to fight at work can be illustrated by making use of the recollections of Kate Adie (2002). She recalled that when she joined the BBC during the 1970s, she entered a business dominated by men and one with relatively few opportunities for women. Working her way up through the regions in both radio and television, she found that she was given human interest stories to cover and was kept away from hard political news stories. This changed, however, when she transferred to London. Here the expectation was that she could work on a range of stories. She spent time covering the royal family, the troubles in Northern Ireland and as a war correspondent. In the early years, however, the confidence granted to her by the editorial team was rarely matched by those working behind the scenes. She recalled that she '. . . hadn't reckoned on the stubbornly neolithic crew room in London, which contained a fair number of beer guts and old hands' (Adie, 2002, p. 108). This was mirrored at times by the opinions of those she interviewed. She noted that trade union leaders and industrialists would often prefer to address their comments to her male cameramen than to deal with a woman journalist. As a woman, she found at times that she wanted to strike out independently and to face dangerous situations alone. She was aware, however, that cultural differences and adverse circumstances made women acceptable targets in some parts of the world. She had friends and colleagues who had experienced sexual harassment and rape whilst attempting to do their jobs, and the problems they encountered made her cautious. She noted in particular that '. . . war zones see most of the usual restrictions on decent behaviour suspended, so nothing can be taken for granted' (Adie, 2002, p. 284). Adie's recollections are hard hitting. It is clear that a difficult job was made even more challenging by the obstructive behaviour of men. Her recollections leave the impression that she spent much of her time on her own, desperate to find new ways to survive in a male-dominated industry.

Divisions between the genders can also be seen in the way that different genders gravitate towards different sectors of employment. Although women are becoming a dominant force in medicine, law, architecture and veterinary medicine, women tend to be underrepresented in senior positions, especially in politics, the judiciary and in town councils (see Sawer and Henry, 2008). Although women dominate the teaching profession, they are less likely to hold senior positions in schools. Research shows that men were more likely to gain the headship of secondary schools, whilst women tend to fare better in primary schools (see McNamara, Howson, Gunter, Sprigade and Onat-Stelma, 2008). Whilst some of the differences in power between men and women could be explained in terms of the choices women make about the way they work, it is also clear that men act as the gatekeepers in some professions and that the advancement of women at work can be limited if the rules of work are set according to the priorities favoured by men.

Conflict with clients

The division between management and workers and between genders are not the only sources of conflict at work. Conflict between workers and their client group is also important. Workers are sometimes subjected to harassment by their clients. In the hospitality trade, for example, women are sometimes subjected to sexual innuendo and unwanted attention from male guests. Although in many cases employers intervene to protect their workers from such behaviour, it is also the case that hotels and restaurants attempt to avoid criticism from their customers and might smooth over disputes between workers and clients (Guerrier and Adib, 2000). Care workers in the not-for-profit sector have reported being subjected to the violent outbursts of their clients. At times these workers find themselves in precarious positions. Their social commitment to care can make them less willing to complain or accuse their clients. Making allowances, care workers can sometimes explain away harsh verbal or physical abuse and claim that such treatment goes with the territory. This can be reinforced amongst colleagues through the use of humour, storytelling and nonchalance; all of which can help the care worker reduce the damage they experience from the abuse (Baines and Cunningham, 2011). People in such circumstances will often have to make a choice between engaging in conflict with their clients, perhaps through making use of formal complaints protocols, or finding ways to minimise the impact of challenging and offensive behaviour on their own lives.

We have seen that conflict is likely to occur at work because of the existence of hierarchies and because of some systemic inequalities between people. Workers can be distinguished from one another by their levels and types of expertise and the extent to which their social identities assist or hinder them in a work setting. We have seen that workers can find themselves disempowered and that this conflicts with the dominant cultural values of freedom and autonomy. Workers can, indeed, find themselves in a confusing position because of having to deal with the imposition of corporate drivers, the demands of management, an inbuilt bias shown towards some groups over others and even demanding and unreasonable clients. This might give the impression, however, that workers are victims of the system and are ultimately powerless. This is far from the truth, as workers will find ways to deal with conflicts and to participate in some forms of resistance.

Resistance

Watson (2012) points out that resistance is often necessary for workers to maintain their own personal integrity and to voice opposition to management attempts to undermine the rights and conditions of employment negotiated by workers and their unions. Collinson (2000) notes that workers can develop different ways to resist the authority and power of management and that this relies upon developing the knowledge and expertise necessary to challenge management. He claims that the development of resistance should be seen as a response to attempts by management to discipline and control rather than as a rationally developed strategy created in the abstract. When we talk about resistance, we need to bear in mind that the methods outlined can apply in a variety of contexts. Direct action, for example, could be advocated in response to systemic inequalities or in response to specific problems arising in a place of work. Workers might be active in the methods they use or might resist through withdrawing cooperation and through the 'banking of enthusiasm' (Hodson, 2001, p. 17). Overt and covert methods could be employed. Although workers will look for the best ways to respond to the problems they encounter, they will not always pull in the same direction. Indeed, individuals will often find their own ways to resist and to survive attempts to place limits upon their lives at work.

Resistance through distance and persistence

Collinson (2000) draws a distinction between *resistance through distance* and *resistance through persistence*. Resistance through distance involves '. . . seeking to secure a degree of personal discretion and autonomy in and around the edges of their formally controlled and commodified position' (Collinson, 2000, p. 171). Rather than take an interest in the running of an organisation, workers can separate their life at work from their life at home to such an extent that they create the necessary distance to disengage and resist the authority of management. Although resistance through distance does relatively little to challenge the hierarchy in any real sense, it can be seen as a way for workers to escape and maintain their own sense of self. In manufacturing industry, this can provide '. . . temporary relief from the incessant pressures and insecurities of shopfloor production and subordination' (Collinson, 2000, p. 173). This differs significantly from *resistance through persistence*, which relies upon developing an understanding of the workplace and a willingness to take on the employer. This form of resistance is more common amongst white-collar workers. These two forms of resistance operate in very different ways. Whereas *resistance through distance* involves nonengagement with work and can be covert, *resistance through persistence* tends to be quite visible; and this can mean that those who resist in this way need to engage even more so with the politics of work. This distinction will be used when discussing the Marxist, feminist and postmodernist approaches to resistance.

Marxism and resistance

If power relations are primarily economic and consist in the conflict between the owners of the means of production and the workers, it would make sense to resist through industrial or revolutionary activity. Marx (see Marx, 1871) was adamant that the liberation of the working class relied upon the activities of workers themselves rather than through the benevolent legislation developed by the middle classes or the aristocracy. He was in favour of industrial action as long as this was accompanied by workers also seizing political power. For some on the political left, workers should avoid working for reforms through legislation and concentrate instead upon attacking capitalism through the use of strikes. Marxists like William Morris (Morris, 1890) as well as those who borrowed from Marx, such as Georges Sorel (Sorel, 1908), believed that revolutionary activity could be spearheaded by workers engaging in a general strike. It is important to note that for these theorists on the left, industrial activity was seen as a way to undermine the legitimacy of capitalism and to provoke the owners of the means of production (and the political state which protected their interests) into a full-blown class war. It is evident that from a Marxist perspective, resistance through distance is not enough because it fails to challenge existing inequalities in power. Resistance through persistence, especially if this involves the continual undermining of the capitalist system, is far more in tune with the Marxist position.

Feminism and resistance

If power relations are primarily situated in the conflict between genders, then it makes sense for resistance to take place within the realm of sexual politics. Feminists tend to view power and resistance in this way, though they do differ in the way they target problems of discrimination and inequality in the workplace. Liberal feminists work within the confines of the capitalist system and argue that the relative subordination of women at work should be countered through the promotion of equal opportunities (see Lewis, 1992). For socialist feminists, the problem lies in the nature of the capitalist system itself. Because of this, the liberation of women is thought to rely upon undermining capitalism and replacing it with the collective ownership of the means of production (see Coote and Campbell, 1987). For radical feminists, it makes no sense for women to cooperate with men, as men are thought to oppress women and are therefore at the root of the problem. The radical feminist solution to the subordination of women at work is to create women-only companies in which women would have the freedom to express themselves without being constrained by domineering men (see Coote and Campbell, 1987; Rowbotham, 1989). Whereas liberal feminists and socialist feminists seem to embrace the fundamentals of resistance through persistence by calling upon women to work towards either the reform or overthrow of the existing system, radical feminists urge women to withdraw from mainstream patriarchal employers and develop their own ways of working. This could be seen as a form of resistance through distance, at least in terms of refusing to participate in patriarchal organisations.

Postmodernism and resistance

From a postmodernist perspective, power and conflict can be detected in all social relations and are not particularly dependent upon class or gender (see Foucault, 1976). If power relations operate on a local level (between individuals), a case could be made for resistance to take place primarily on a local level. Some form of resistance is needed for power relations to exist. Without resistance, those seeking to exert an influence would lack opposition and would thus not need to stretch their own powers (see Smart, 1985). From a postmodernist perspective, work can be reduced to a game of conflicting power relations. As part of his description of contemporary society as one of liquid modernity, Bauman (2000) claimed that people have become less convinced of the permanence of work and have become more inclined to view work as a game in which they have to concentrate upon the short term and think about the immediate effects of their manoeuvres. Deetz (2000) notes that some people regard work as a game and expend enormous amounts of energy trying to beat the system. This can give rise to the workers becoming '... consumed by staying viable in the game, haunted by the prospect that he or she cannot control the self or others enough to win...' (Deetz, 2000, p. 159). For those who regard work as a game, class or gender divisions do not particularly matter. What does matter is that people understand how power is used to control their behaviour and how they can resist. This does not necessarily mean being overt in their resistance. Resistance could be through withdrawal, subterfuge and through creating a sense of distance. Resistance through distance thus becomes a possible postmodern response to power relations at work.

The importance of the group in resistance

Whilst individuals might expend a lot of energy in finding ways to resist management and register their opposition to their conditions of employment, the group is important in witnessing resistance and in giving resistance meaning beyond the immediate act. Watson (2012) provides a number of interesting examples of how workers use humour to maintain their own integrity and show some solidarity with their colleagues. Workers in a blind making factory, for example, attributed special significance to a song entitled "We've Got to Get out of This Place" as it captured their own sentiments. Workers might also share their disdain for awkward customers by devising their own shorthand terms to describe them. An example is provided of chip shop workers who referred to some of their customers as SUBs, which stands for soaking up the beer. Those who buy and sell stolen goods at work will often look beyond the mere financial transaction and view the deal as a social transaction between friends and trusted colleagues. These examples show the importance of registering opposition, even if this is sometimes quite symbolic, as a way for workers to express unity with others and to distance themselves from the mundane routine of their work. Whilst some of the behaviour might be wicked, cutting or illegal, it can serve as a useful safety value at work and help to prevent tension overflowing into the relationships between colleagues.

5a. Students on resisting power in bar work

Students tend to have the experience of working in low-skilled occupations where they have relatively little power to resist. For some, power can be resisted by finding ways to avoid surveillance. Laura talked about how she would meet her colleagues in areas of the pub in which she worked where there were no cameras and how this allowed them to feel as if they were resisting power (Laura).

We can see that systemic inequalities between different classes and genders give rise to different forms of resistance as exemplified by Marxist and feminist strategies. Even within these ideological envelopes, there is still plenty of room for variety and for the evolution of different strategies over time. Although industrial activity is one of the most common forms of resistance, workers might also choose to pull out of capitalist hierarchies to develop alternative ways of working, or they might stay in these organisations and develop coping strategies or games necessary to maintain their sanity. Whilst it is clear that workers have a choice between compliance and

learning about work

overt or covert resistance, it remains contentious whether resistance requires a public display in order to be effective. Is it necessary for the employer and management to be aware that workers are resisting or is it enough for workers to know that they are giving less than they are able? The problem with attempting to quantify resistance is that it will tend to record *resistance through persistence* rather than *resistance through distance*. Indeed, resistance through distance could easily be interpreted as compliance by employers and management and this might in turn have a dramatic impact on the way they choose to manage change. As we will see in the next section, resistance is an important dimension of change management.

Change management

Change is often unavoidable because of the pressure of the market, strategic drivers in organisations and even the fragility of the egos of management. Regardless of the reasons for change, managers will encounter resistance from at least some pockets of the workers. Dechawatanapaisal and Siengthai (2006) claim that people tend to hold on to knowledge that supports their particular view of the world and can be resistant to knowledge that threatens to destabilise their core values. The extent to which they resist will depend upon the strength of their existing commitment to a particular view of the legitimate remit of their work. The reluctance of people to be drawn out of their comfort zone creates a considerable challenge to managers, who often need to devise ways to energise workers and to encourage them to think freshly about their views on the work they do. Moore (2007) claims that one of the main barriers to change is a reluctance to consider alternative ways of working and that the development of creativity, critical thinking and reflective powers at work could contribute towards a more conducive climate in which the complexities of change are considered. Although it is important for change managers to attempt to build a consensus in support of change, they must avoid focusing too much upon the possible benefits and failing to give due weight to possible drawbacks (see Folger and Skarlicki, 1999). Managing change involves developing a clear rationale for change, preparing the workers for these changes and taking into account possible lines of resistance.

Creating readiness for change

Change applied without warning and without taking into account the opinions of workers is unlikely to be popular. Self (2007) argues that organisations need to create readiness to change and that this can help to reduce possible resistance. Change can be justified by pointing out that the product or service on offer is no longer suitable for the market, that the proposed changes are likely to be more profitable, that the management team has experience in instituting change successfully and that key stakeholders support the proposed changes. Aladwani (2001) likewise claims that resistance to change can be alleviated through communicating the benefits of innovation, by illustrating the implications of the change as clearly as possible, by showing that the change would be cost effective, through illustrating that the quality of the service or product would improve and by showing that key individuals in an organisation support the need to change. These contributions to the debate approach the issue by asking what management can do to overcome resistance. There is, however, another way to look at this which involves incorporating resistance into the way change is managed.

Change management and resistance

It is important for managers to realise there are good reasons for workers to resist the imposition of change. If workers feel under threat, they understandably become far more vigilant and interpret managerial interventions in a negative light. Resistance involves challenging the existing power structure and the discourse is used to justify these power relations (see Folger and Skarlicki, 1999). Traditionally, resistance is viewed as being detrimental to an organisation and a sign of a dysfunctional culture at work (see Waddell and Sohal, 1998). Folger and Skarlicki (1999) point out that when workers feel they are being treated unfairly, strategies of resistance and resentments develop, which are in turn mobilised to resist changes imposed by employers. Because of this, it is argued that '. . . organisational fairness is a psychological mechanism that can mediate employee resistance to change' (Folger and Skarlicki, 1999, p. 36). Management needs to recognise, moreover, that some forms of resistance can be beneficial to organisations by highlighting when proposed changes are flawed and counterproductive (Folger and Skarlicki, 1999). Waddell and Sohal (1998) point out that resistance can be a stabilising factor by placing limits upon the constant demand for change. Workers who resist often do so in response to the perceived uncertainties that change can create. Resistance can also push organisations to consider proposed changes with care, knowing that they will have to fight to bring about changes in practice. Apathy, conversely, will allow changes to be devised and implemented without due care. Whilst resistance for resistance sake might be damaging to an organisation and to relations between management and workers, resistance which recognises the need for constructive change can have its benefits.

Resistance to change in teaching

The attitudes of workers towards change will be influenced by the way their view their own careers. Vahasantanen and Billett (2008), for example, interviewed 16 teachers in Finland to investigate their attitudes towards change in their profession. Teachers voiced concern over rapid change because it can undermine the professional status of teachers, erode their motivation and have a negative impact upon their relationship with students. Although some teachers will accept changes imposed without question, others will find ways to resist change or at least consider when it is best to cooperate or to resist. They found that teachers who were committed to their own professional development tended to adopt positive attitudes towards change. For many teachers, however, change was seen as a potential threat. Whilst some teachers voiced their concerns over the possible impact upon their working lives, others adopted more critical attitudes and argued that constant change within education created problems for students and undermined the professional commitment of teachers. Although this research is based upon a relatively small sample, it is useful in illustrating how attitudes towards change are often shaped by broader concerns about careers and about the importance of continuing professional development. Workers who hope to remain stationary in terms of their skills and their roles at work are more likely to regard the prospects of change as threatening and will tend to view proposals for change in a negative light.

We have seen that widespread preference for the familiar can create a significant barrier to change. Attitudes towards change are also influenced by existing views about management and approaches to one's own professional development. If an organisation is seen to provide the context and opportunities for a worker's own development, resistance is less likely than if the organisation is regarded as oppressive and restrictive of one's life as a worker. Although it is possible for workers to take part in the change process by voicing their opposition and resistance to ill thought out plans, their effectiveness will depend a great deal upon patterns of leadership and decision making at work. These issues will be covered in more detail in part two of this book.

Conclusion

Understanding how conflict and resistance operate at work can help place the methods used to control behaviour in a broader context. Managers have a vested interest in minimising conflict in the workplace and will often attempt to find ways to unite workers and secure their interest and support for the strategic aims of the employer. Failure to create unity, alongside deeply ingrained divisions, will lead employers to search for ways to contain resentments and manage conflict. Workers will often respond to interventions from management by developing the ways they resist. This could be necessary to deal with the frustrations and negative emotions generated in work. It can involve increased engagement with the politics of work, perhaps through becoming more involved in trade union activity or through membership in work-based committees. Some people might prefer to disengage from work and everything it stands for. A person working for a cable or satellite TV company, for example, could refuse to have this in his or her own home and coast through their work with little regard for the product they provide. People who are alienated in their work will often find ways to resist their employers, whilst those who are more fulfilled at work may well buy into the corporate message or at least find pockets of autonomy to make their work have meaning. Whilst employers might talk about brand and common sacrifice, workers will require respect or find ways to resist. This resistance might take place in opposition to injustices and in response to inbuilt inequalities at work. It might also be expressed in response to management attempts to impose change. Rather than see resistance as dysfunctional and unacceptable, it makes sense for management to attempt to understand the origins of dissatisfaction at work and to address, wherever possible, problems identified by the workers. Apart from anything else, it will allow management to view their own proposals in a critical light and iron out problems in the planning stage rather than face a hostile reception when change is introduced.

Questions to consider

1. To what extent is conflict at work unavoidable?
2. How useful is the distinction between *resistance through persistence* and *resistance through distance*?
3. How important is resistance in the management of change?

A guide to reading

For general accounts of conflict at work, Watson (2012) and Beck (2000) provide interesting introductions. Collinson (2000), Hodson (2001) and Watson (2012) provide an outline of the importance of resistance at work. The foundations of the Marxist approach can be found in Marx and Engels (1848) and Marx (1871). Lewis (1992), Coote and Campbell (1987) and Rowbotham (1989) approach conflict and resistance from a feminist point of view. Postmodern perspectives can be traced in Bauman (2000) and Deetz (2000). Whilst Self (2007) and Aladwani (2001) approach change management from the point of view of management, Folger and Skarlicki (1999) and Waddell and Sohal (1998) recognise that resistance from workers can assist in the development of a coherent approach to change.

References

Adie, K. (2002) *The Kindness of Strangers*, Headline Book Publishing: London.
Aladwani, A. (2001) 'Change management strategies for successful ERP implementation', *Business Process Management Journal*, Volume 7, Issue 3, pp. 266–275.

Baines, D. and Cunningham, I. (2011) 'White knuckle care work:Violence, gender and new public management in the voluntary sector', *Work, Employment & Society*,Volume 25, Issue 4, pp.760–776.

Bauman, Z. (2000) *Liquid Modernity*, Polity: Cambridge.

Beck, U. (2000) *The Brave New World of Work*, Polity Press: Cambridge.

Blair, T. (2010) *A Journey*, Arrow Books: London.

Collinson, D. (2000) 'Resistance'. In K. Grint (ed) (2000) *Work and Society: A Reader*, Polity: Cambridge, pp. 163–195.

Coote, A. and Campbell, B. (1987) *Sweet Freedom*, Basil Blackwell: London.

Dechawatanapaisal, D. and Siengthai, S. (2006) 'The impact of cognitive dissonance on learning work behaviour', *Journal of Workplace Learning*,Volume 18, Issue 1, pp. 42–54.

Deetz, S. 'Discipline'. In K. Grint (ed) (2000) *Work and Society: A Reader*, Polity: Cambridge, pp. 142–162.

Folger, R. and Skarlicki, D. (1999) 'Unfairness and resistance to change: Hardship as mistreatment', *Journal of Organisational Change Management*, Volume 12, Issue 1, pp. 35–50.

Foucault, M. (1976) 'Two lectures'. In C. Gordon (ed) (1980) *Michel Foucault: Power/Knowledge*, Harvester Wheatsheaf: New York, 1980, pp. 78–108.

Fram, E. and McCarthy, M. (2003), 'From employee to brand champion', *Marketing Management*,Volume 12, Issue 1, p. 25.

Grobel, L. (ed) (2006) *Al Pacino in Conversation with Lawrence Grobel*, Pocket Books: London.

Guerrier, Y. and Adib, A. S. (2000) 'No we don't provide that service: The harassment of hotel employees by customers', *Work, Employment & Society*,Volume 14, Issue 4, pp. 689–705.

Hodson, R. (2001) *Dignity at Work*, Cambridge University Press: Cambridge.

Lewis, J. (1992) *Women in Britain Since 1945*, Blackwell: Oxford.

Marx, K. (1871) 'The Civil War in France'. In K. Marx and F. Engels (eds) (1977) *Selected Works*, Lawrence and Wishart: London, pp. 271–307.

Marx, K. and Engels, F. (1848) 'Manifesto of the Communist Party'. In K. Marx and F. Engels (eds) (1977) *Selected Works*, Lawrence and Wishart: London, pp. 31–63.

McNamara, O., Howson, J., Gunter, H., Sprigade, A. and Onat-Stelma, Z. (2008) *Women Teachers' Careers*, NASUWT: Birmingham.

Moore, L. (2007) 'Ethical and organisational tensions for work-based learners', *Journal of Workplace Learning*,Volume 19, Issue 3, pp. 161–172.

Morris, W. (1890) 'News from nowhere'. In C. Wilmer (ed) (1993) *News From Nowhere and Other Writings*, Penguin: London, pp. 41–230.

Ransome, P. (1999) *Sociology and the Future of Work*, Ashgate: Aldershot.

Rowbotham, S. (1989) *The Past Is Before Us*, Pandora: London.

Sawer, P. and Henry, J. (2008) 'How women will take over the workplace; investigation; teamwork, leadership, communication, emotional intelligence', *The Sunday Telegraph*, 12 October 2008, p. 12.

Self, D. (2007), 'Organisational change – overcoming resistance by creating readiness', *Development and Learning in Organisations: An International Journal*.Volume 21, Issue 5, pp. 11–13.

Smart, B. (1985) *Michel Foucault*, Tavistock: London.

Sorel, G. (1908) *Reflections on Violence*, Cambridge University Press: Cambridge, 1999 edition.

Vahasantanen, K. and Billett, S. (2008) 'Negotiating professional identity'. In S. Billett, C. Harteis and A. Etelapelto (2008) (eds) *Emerging Perspectives of Workplace Learning*, Sense Publishers: Rotterdam, pp. 35–49.

Waddell, D. and Sohal, A. (1998) 'Resistance: A constructive tool for change management', *Management Decision*, Volume 36, Issue 8, pp. 543–548.

Waldregrave, W. (2010) 'All you need is guile, sensitivity and rhino skin', *The Times*, 1 June 2010, p. 21.

Watson, T. (2003) *Sociology, Work and Industry*, Routledge: London.

Watson, T. (2012) *Sociology, Work and Organisation*, Routledge: Oxon.

White, D. (2003) 'People power drives Asda's push for top colleague culture is producing a motivated team and a growing market share', *The Daily Telegraph*, 20 November 2003, p. 9.

learning about work

chapter 6

Social Capital, Community and Social Responsibility

In addition to being individuals and associating with others in relations of power, people are also members of communities. Communities will contain social capital of one sort or another, which is another way of saying that a community can be characterised by the links between people. These links give communities their distinctive atmosphere or personality. One of the key ways of interacting with the community is through work. By working with others in the community, people gain both an insight into the community itself and have some impact upon its character. The extent to which people can influence others will vary according to the work they do, but people will often pick up a great deal about the community from living and working alongside others. In this chapter, we take a look at the importance of social capital, community and social responsibility to those who seek to intervene in the community through their work. Examples from teaching, the police, social work and the voluntary sector will be used to illustrate how professionals can be shaped by the social capital of a community and by their active dialogue with residents and their involvement in social projects. By focusing upon these social concepts, we discover another way to view the dynamic identity of workers and the work process.

Social capital

Social capital can be seen as the measure of trust in society. At least some level of social capital is necessary for people to cooperate in collective endeavours, and it should be evident that the absence of social capital would make such cooperation virtually impossible. Social capital is an essential feature of economic, social and political life. Instead of concentrating solely upon the relationship and relative power of the individual vis-à-vis the state, those who are interested in social capital recognise that the individual is far from an abstraction and that people associate with one another in communities. For those who see society in this way, social capital is something to be valued highly (see Alcock, 2000; Rodger, 2000; Todd and Taylor, 2004). The idea of social capital has many attractions, perhaps because it provides an alternative to the stark world view in which people are relegated or reduced to producers and consumers.

We begin the discussion of social capital by taking a look at the ideas of Pierre Bourdieu and his useful distinction between economic, social and cultural capital. Bourdieu (1986) noted that economic capital lies at the foundation of other forms of capital and that economic capital is effectively transformed and disguised by other forms of capital. Although he did not want to overemphasise the importance of economics, he argued that the possession of sufficient economic capital allowed people to cultivate both their social capital and their cultural capital. He traced social capital to the '. . . possession of more or less institutionalized relationships of mutual acquaintance and recognition – or in other words, to membership in a group – which provides each of its members with the backing of the collectively-owned capital. . .' (Bourdieu, 1986, p. 51). The amount of social capital people have is thought to depend upon the extent of their networks and is maintained as a series of relationships. Cultural capital, finally, consists in a person's aesthetic appreciation and internal life. This can be cultivated through individual effort but is also transmitted through family background and the education system. For Bourdieu, economic, social and cultural capital provide the foundation of the class system.

The concept of social capital has been developed further in the writings of Robert Putnam and Francis Fukuyama. Putnam (2000) describes social capital as '. . . connections among individuals – social networks and the norms of reciprocity and trustworthiness that arise from them' (Putnam, 2000, p. 19). As with physical and human capital, it is seen to have inherent value arising from the networks between people which allow for greater productivity amongst groups and individuals. Social capital can benefit individuals by forging useful connections and can benefit the community by facilitating collective action. For Fukuyama (1995), social capital is dependent on the levels of trust in society. This includes all groups from the family unit to the nation-state. It originates and continues to develop though religion, tradition and values. Social capital is not something that can be bought. Rather, it rests upon the acquisition of social virtues and manifests itself in a culture which places high value upon honesty, loyalty and service to others. In the case of both Putnam and Fukuyama, social capital is viewed as something that can enrich the individual and the community. Not only does it provide some rules for behaviour, it is also the link between individuals that makes cooperation possible within the community. It serves to remind people that they can serve their own interests as well as those of the broader collective. As we will see, the links between people can be important in the workplace and for the economy as a whole.

Social capital and finding work

Social capital can help an individual to find work. Putnam (2000) argues that a person's economic success is often influenced by the extent and scope of his or her social networks. People from affluent families with influential social ties can utilise these links in order to succeed in the marketplace. Conversely, people from economically disadvantaged areas are often hampered by the absence of the financial and educational resources necessary to advance and the social ties needed to acquire other forms of capital. Indeed, it is argued that '. . . social capital is a powerful resource for achieving occupational advancement, social status, and economic rewards' (Putnam, 2000, p. 321). On a practical level, social networks can offer advice, information and potential job opportunities. Field (2003) suggests that the practice of relying on friends and family when searching for work has long provided an effective way of helping individuals to find new jobs and to prosper in work. It is estimated that the influence of personal contacts accounts for approximately 55% of successful job applications for graduate-level employment (Snowdon, 2010). Although professional network sites like LinkedIn provide people with an opportunity to advertise their skills and attract the attention of employers (see Warman, 2014), people are still urged to use friends and family as a foundation for their contact lists and to gain introductions through these personal connections (see Bridge, 2010). The development of digital communities might increase the range of contacts people have, but they should not be seen as being more important than the networks they develop through family and friends.

Trust at work

The way people experience work can often be influenced by the levels of trust exhibited between workers. Fukuyama (1995) notes that the workplace allows people to move within social circles outside of their private lives. Whilst the need to earn money remains, the workplace is an important arena for human activity partly because people often want to feel a part of a larger social group. Within the workplace, social capital allows people to operate on the basis of trust and shared values, thus reducing the need for rules and regulations. This can lead to greater innovation and higher levels of fulfilment in work as social relationships are formed and expanded and responsibilities extended throughout the organisation. Conversely, lower levels of trust will tend to make it necessary to exert more control over the workforce. Some organisations will employ occupational psychologists to intervene and to suggest ways to enhance trust in the workplace. Russell (2014) claims that a low level of trust at work creates a culture where workers become preoccupied with the agendas and intentions of their colleagues and where they fear making mistakes in case these are used against them. Mistakes made are therefore concealed and a culture of blame is fuelled. She argues that levels of trust can be improved by colleagues sharing personal histories, through team-building exercises to stretch workers both physically and mentally and through the use of personality tests to reveal similarities and differences between colleagues. These methods are advocated in the belief that workers become more efficient in a trusting environment and that knowledge of one another can promote empathy and respect for the skills each person can bring to the workplace.

Social capital and the economy

Decent levels of social capital can be beneficial for the economy, partly because enhancing levels of trust at work can make workers more productive. When this is applied to the economy as a whole, the benefits can become even more evident. Fukuyama (1995) argues against the view that the economy is a separate entity which operates under its own rules outside the influence of wider society. In his view, the economy is one of the prime arenas for human interaction. Fukuyama claims that the economy benefits from greater collaboration between people and that the '. . . greatest economic efficiency was not necessarily achieved by rational self-interested individuals but rather by groups of individuals who, because of a pre-existing moral community, are able to work together effectively' (Fukuyama, 1995, p. 21). This social or moral dimension would seem to be lacking in free market economics. According to Kuttner (1996), free market economics can undermine social capital and commitment to the community. He notes that the pressures of the free market will force companies to pay more attention to profit margins and less to the welfare of the community. This in turn undermines individual and corporate responsibility. By polarising incomes and increasing economic insecurity, the free market is thought to decrease the amount of time and energy people have to participate in civic life. The arguments outlined earlier illustrate that building social capital can improve economic performance by helping to create a more cooperative culture at work and that the naked pursuit of profit is often at the expense of developing trust and commitment at work. This can drain workers and make them less willing to participate in the life of the community. The way people experience work can influence not only their attitudes towards their colleagues but also the way they see their own social responsibilities.

Social capital and fulfilment

Social capital can also influence levels of fulfilment at work. Alison Eadie (2001) identified some of the reasons why people are unable to attain fulfilment in their lives. Although many people are materially more comfortable than in the past, they can still find themselves unfulfilled. She claims that the decline of social capital resulting from reduced participation in church, political associations and social groups has left many people feeling isolated. In her view, the search for meaning experienced by many people cannot be remedied by work alone. Instead, she argued that broader social needs are best met by activities outside of the workplace through relationships, hobbies, voluntary work and community activity. For those who argue in this way, it would appear that fulfilment is not something that can be attained by the isolated individual. Although some people might be fortunate enough to find fulfilling work, this will not necessarily be enough unless it is also accompanied by some enriching social relationships. These might be formed in the workplace, through shared social activities or in the broader community.

The idea of social capital is important because it shows how society relies heavily upon the organic connections between people and that these can be formed through social interactions and do not rely upon being imposed from above. Social capital is also usefully located alongside economic and cultural capital in a way that allows us to see different facets of a person's identity. Rather than explore the issues of dwindling social capital and its relationship to the decline in popular participation in community groups, this section on social capital has focused primarily upon the importance of social capital for finding work, establishing one's place in work and for the smooth running of the capitalist economy. It is important to note, however, that social capital can be viewed as a tool necessary to sustain inequalities in society. In itself it does little to challenge these inequalities and it could be said to divert attention away from systemic problems by encouraging people to find ways to nurture their social networks for the benefit of all.

Community

A distinction can be made between moral and social views of the community. The moral view concentrates upon the ways that communities can be bound by a shared set of values. Religious principles, for example, can give a community a shared sense of identity. This fairly conservative view of the community is used to justify the suppression of opinions that are deemed to threaten the unity of the community (see Jeffries, 1996; Perry, 1993). The social view of the community is associated far more with liberal opinion. Communities can be seen to evolve to serve definite social needs and rely upon the active participation of their members for their growth and prosperity. Viewing the community in this way goes hand in hand with the notion of active citizenship and the belief that individuals also benefit from promoting the good of others. This line of argument owes a great deal to the influence of Aristotle and Rousseau and can be seen in the ideas of modern communitarians (see Aristotle, 1912; Kymlicka, 2002; Rousseau, 1968). The social view of the community provides a backbone to the notion of social capital and a focal point for those who seek to enrich the links between members of the community.

Social capital and the community

Key theorists of social capital recognise that levels of social capital tend to be higher where people take an active part in their communities. Fukuyama (1995) pointed out that rampant individualism can have a negative impact upon society by giving rise to higher crime rates, increased litigation and can contribute towards the decline in family, community activity and membership of social groups. According to Putnam (2000), neighbourhoods with higher levels of social capital tend to have cleaner public spaces, friendlier people and safer streets. Moreover, neighbourhoods with high levels of social capital are more likely to prove popular places to live and have residents who vote, belong to neighbourhood groups and value their surroundings. The idea of social capital provides a way to understand the ways in which the character of communities changes over time. It can serve as a focal point for community workers and for those interested in social reform by alerting them to the connection between poor levels of social capital and a range of social problems. If social problems can be traced to poor levels of social capital, it would make sense for the government to invest in projects to develop social capital and to focus some of its efforts on building up the social networks and personality of the community in this way. Approaching social problems in this way could, however, miss the point by attributing far too much to the influence of the community and far too little to the responsibilities of the individual or to systemic inequalities.

The transformation of community

The idea of community involvement has an important place in radical social theory. Beck (2000), for example, claims that the idea of the traditional community which naturally evolves for no particular reason should be sidelined and replaced by the notion of a risk community in which people join together to defend themselves against a variety of dangers. These risk communities are not confined to small geographical areas but can cut across national boundaries. Beck is an advocate of redistributing work, relying less upon paid employment and encouraging people to voluntarily take on civil labour. This work could be paid for by civic money and be seen as an alternative to some welfare benefits. In his view, people might engage in civil labour alongside traditional paid work as '. . . an alternative source of activity and identity which not only gives people satisfaction, but also creates cohesion in individualised society by breathing life into everyday democracy' (Beck, 2000, p. 127). Making use of civil labour was seen as one way to energise the community. Some sections of the Green movement (see Taylor, 2007) likewise argue in favour of reducing reliance upon paid work and encouraging people to dedicate more of their time to community activity. This is advocated in the belief that people could become more fulfilled and happy if they spent less of their time chasing financial rewards and dedicated more of their time to the welfare of their local community. This is by no means pure philanthropy. The social view of the community shows the connection between the welfare of the community and personal welfare. By dedicating some time to improving the physical and social environment, social capital could be enhanced and the individual could benefit. This only makes sense, however, to those who believe in the interconnectedness of individuals and who believe that the community provides not merely a home for individuals but also has a direct impact upon their social makeup and value system.

Volunteering and social divisions

Volunteering and taking part in community groups can help to reduce social divisions by including people from different classes and occupational backgrounds. The extent to which this occurs, however, depends upon the class characteristics of a particular area. In the United States, voluntary groups in New Hampshire include people across the classes. In the south-west of America, however, voluntary groups tend to be dominated by professionals (Lewin, 2001). When talking about volunteering in the United States, Putnam (2000) notes that people with a good education, financial stability and wide social networks are more likely to volunteer and remain committed to volunteering for a number of years, whilst those who are socially isolated are much less likely to give time or money to community ventures. Paula Span (2005) noted that although people might be reluctant to join organisations, informal networks in the United States help to bring people together and to deal with some of the disintegration of inner-city communities. In her view, people do not want to live in a community of strangers and often feel safer when they make connections with others. Field (2003) claims that volunteering in the United Kingdom is primarily carried out by the middle classes. Although the work undertaken by voluntary groups may help to facilitate contact between people from different backgrounds, it is also the case that the dominance of the middle classes may exacerbate inequalities. The Labour government of 1997–2010 was particularly interested in attracting older members of the community to voluntary service. It was argued that young people in deprived areas would benefit greatly from being mentored by retired teachers, people from the business community and health professionals (see Bennett, 2001). Whilst volunteering has the potential to bring different sections of society together and serve as a form of social education for all concerned, it is clear that volunteering tends to attract a relatively small section of society who have the financial security, energy and free time to give to others. The argument that volunteering builds social capital is thus open to some criticism, especially if volunteering attracts relatively small pockets of society. It might mean, indeed, that volunteering reinforces a particular view of the community and attracts those who view communities in this way. If this is the case, there is no reason to believe that their actions will be welcomed by all sections of a community and that their motives will be understood and appreciated as intended.

Students and community involvement

Crick (1998) highlighted the importance of students taking part in their local communities. Community involvement provides an arena for students to engage with the community either through work-related learning in community groups or through coming into contact with diverse sections of the community. By working in the community, students can gain a better understanding of the connections they have with other people and their rights and responsibilities as citizens. By joining with others to deal with social issues, students will recognise increasingly that being a citizen is not a static status defined purely in terms of legal rights, but involves a dynamic process through which people help to mould their communities through their actions (see also Taylor, Mellor and Walton, 2009). Community involvement can provide students with valuable social education and help to develop a range of skills. Fiona Christie (2005) claims that volunteering can do a great deal to enhance the CVs of students, develop their skill base and broaden their horizons by allowing them scope to participate constructively in their local communities. It should be noted, however, that students should be able to glean something about their communities through participating in many forms of work (see box 6a).

The importance of community for the professions

The community provides a context for many professions. Each community will have its own dominant characteristics and its own set of networks which help to form its social capital. Many communities are diverse and some struggle to find ways to live in relative harmony. Professionals involved in working with the community need to understand what makes their community tick. If they are to intervene effectively in the lives of others, they need to do so as a result of their knowledge of the community rather than as a result of their own particular social and cultural capital. Professionals are thus faced with a choice between isolating themselves from the community in which they work or integrating as best they can. They can cultivate the persona of an outsider or seek, through their involvement in the community, a more detailed appreciation of what needs to be done and what they are able to offer. This can be illustrated by making use of examples from teaching and social work.

Teaching

Those who embark upon a career in teaching must recognise that they do not educate children in isolation of a wide range of cultural factors. In order to communicate with their pupils effectively, it is important for teachers to have some understanding of the culture of their communities. Dr Patrick Roach (2009) has argued that schools should take an active interest in community cohesion. Schools are thought to have an important role in fostering tolerance and understanding diversity in the community. Roach claims that the education process requires schools to work together with other services in the community to meet the needs of children. Based upon a series of interviews with teachers and parents at a primary school in the United States, Reed (2009) concluded that where teachers live in the communities in which they teach, they are able to gain a more intimate knowledge of the social and cultural background of the children at their schools. Teachers living locally are more likely to interact with children and their families outside of school and this tends to be viewed in a positive light by many parents. Teachers who commute, on the other hand, are often seen as having less knowledge of, and commitment to, the local community. Reed notes that teachers who live locally '. . . enter classrooms with a network of local relationships, cultural knowledge of students and families, and a contextualised understanding of the neighbourhood and what it means to live there' (Reed, 2009, p. 69). Parental involvement in schools has been shown to be particularly important in tackling social deprivation. Brooks (2009) noted how bringing parents into a school in a deprived area to observe and comment upon lessons and to support the school in a variety of campaigns helped to dismantle some of the barriers between the school and the local community and improved parental involvement in the education of their children. The benefits of this were by no means one way. By cultivating the active participation of parents in their children's education, teachers also found that they gained considerable knowledge of their community and were able to use this insight in their teaching.

Building bridges between schools and the community can be a complicated and delicate process. It is not simply a case of finding spaces for members of the community to have their say but also finding ways to facilitate mutually beneficial cultural exchanges. Ryan (2002) interviewed 35 principals from two diverse Canadian school districts in order to explore the ways in which communities were included in the running of schools. For the most part, involvement was focused on partnerships and collaborations. The first contact was often initiated by the school and this set the terms and conditions of the relationship with the community. Establishing good relationships with the community was considered necessary for the school to pass on information, whilst at the same time getting to know more about the surrounding area. Ryan points out that the development of these connections, especially with parents, helped to narrow the gap between the school and the community and improve the performance of children at school. He was convinced that '. . . professional teaching practice needs to be inclusive, that is, it must incorporate a range of diverse community knowledge, practices and values' (Ryan, 2002, p. 19). This can be seen as an illustration of how working in education can enhance the way the community is viewed. For education to be effective and relevant, it makes sense for teachers to embrace community involvement in the education process and to recognise that gaining knowledge of their own communities can help teachers become more effective in their work. Although this might seem rather instrumental, it is no doubt the case that teachers will sometimes struggle to understand the cultural capital of the children they teach. Finding ways to deal with this deficit must surely be important for those who are seeking to communicate with a diverse range of people.

Social work

Knowledge of the communities in which they work is essential for social workers to intervene effectively. Whilst social workers need to be client-focused and mindful of the specific needs of their clients, they also work in specific communities which will have their own particular characteristics. Ungar, Manuel, Mealey, Thomas and Campbell (2004) conducted a series of interviews with non-professional community helpers and showed how these workers often benefitted from their ties with the local community and were able to have a positive impact on their neighbours. By contrast, the authors of the study claimed that social workers were encouraged too often to remain detached from the community and to maintain a professional distance from their client group. Drawing upon the successes of the community helpers, they called for social workers to reflect upon the wisdom of cultivating an outsider status and consider the benefits of becoming more involved in the life of the community. In their view, it was important for social workers to '. . . reposition themselves with and in the communities they serve' (Ungar et al., 2004, p. 550). As with teaching, this process can be two way. Social workers can gain an understanding of the community and a foothold with local residents by playing a more active role in the communities in which they work. The question social workers need to ask themselves is whether cultivating this understanding is more important than maintaining a professional distance. Perhaps there is a fragile line here between creating sufficient distance to protect their own identity and privacy and immersing themselves enough to be able to empathise and understand the needs of their client group. Although individual social workers need to be able to determine how far they wish to be involved in their communities, having some knowledge of the benefits of community involvement and the limits created by professional detachment would seem important.

One of the key functions of a social worker is to work with individuals and communities in developing their abilities to manage their own affairs. This has become increasingly evident since the 1990s when governments in many Western democracies began to withdraw from the direct provision of social support and started to talk more about empowering communities. In the United States, for example, social workers have been urged to embrace community practice which involves '. . . work with individuals, task groups, organisations, and communities to produce positive social outcomes in neighbourhoods, human services, and communities' (Weil, 1996, pp. 490–491). Weil (1996) insisted that social work has a key part to play in empowering communities and individuals and in the fight for social justice through encouraging the development of leadership skills amongst community members. According to Weil, it is important for social workers to '. . . understand their responsibilities as intermediaries and work with the factors and values that are critical for the survival of democratic societies; this work needs to take place at the family, community, and inter-organisational levels' (Weil, 1996, p. 487). It should be clear that social work is rarely about giving something to the community but about helping individuals and the community to develop their own capacity. By engaging in this work, social workers will deal with diverse sections of the community and will need to place themselves within a network of relationships with individuals, community groups and other agencies. This can no doubt be traced to the influence of policies deliberately designed to limit the remit of the welfare state and to encourage people to take more responsibility for their own lives. Within this framework, social workers take on an important role in urging people to become more self-reliant and less dependent upon the welfare system. In this way, social workers become agents of the community rather than of the state.

Problems with community involvement

Being motivated by the best of intentions does not guarantee success in community work. It is worth bearing in mind that communities do not necessarily treat all members equally and that even the most politically correct communities will have insiders and outsiders. Philip Gold (2000, 2003) notes that the desire to enhance social capital and build communities can sometimes fail to take into account the oppressive and intolerant sides of communities. Halpern (2005) claims that communities with high levels of social capital can sometimes become less understanding of people and places outside of their own environment. The uneven development of social capital can indeed exacerbate social divisions and create problems for excluded pockets in society for '. . . members of the communities concerned may continue to be excluded from networks that could link them back into the wider society, boost the aspirations and attainments of their children, and link adults back into employment' (Halpern, 2005, p. 290). Empowering communities does not necessarily mean that there will be greater levels of equality between their members or that all members will feel more involved in changes taking place in their area. As we will see, successful intervention in communities can also be hampered by the predispositions of those professionals concerned. This can be illustrated with examples from the police and the voluntary sector.

Police

Building sustainable relationships with the community has become an important part of police work, though what needs to be done to build these relationships is far from straightforward. Terpstra (2009) argues that whilst these relationships are important, they can sometimes create problems with enforcing the law and can lead members of the community to expect police officers to work out of hours. Based upon research conducted in the Netherlands, Terpstra argues that police officers must be clear about what they expect from the community; especially if this extends beyond providing officers with information. Failure to be clear about this is thought to jeopardise the relationship between members of the police force and the community. Similar problems have been identified with community policing in the United States. Chappell (2009) noted that although there is widespread support amongst police officers for the principles of community involvement, they often feel there is insufficient training and resources available for this proactive approach to policing. Police officers find they have to prioritise law enforcement over building relationships with the community and that involvement in community initiatives can only ever be a small part of the job. In a survey involving police officers in the Midwest of the United States, Yim and Schafer (2009) noted that police officers often assume that they are viewed negatively by the community, even when this is not the case. Attempts by police officers to uphold a positive image in the community is potentially damaged if they believe that the community views them negatively. Indeed, it is argued that police officers '. . . may not be able to effectively perform their roles as service providers and crime fighters because of this perceived negative regard' (Yim and Schafer, 2009, p. 26). Police officers can thus struggle to find the right balance between community involvement and upholding the law. Whilst community involvement can be seen to build bridges between the police force and the community, its success relies upon goodwill on both sides and perhaps upon police officers feeling valued in their communities. Herein lies the roots of frustration. It is one thing to say that community policing can help to develop the social capital of deprived areas, it is quite another to say that what the police have to offer those areas is consistent with the cultural values of those communities. This would seem to suggest effective community policing relies upon understanding and building upon the existing social capital of a community, rather than attempting to transplant a different set of cultural values upon a potentially unreceptive community.

Voluntary sector

The social background of voluntary sector workers can create obstacles to effective intervention in marginalised communities. Indeed, there is often a mismatch between service providers and the communities in which they serve. Part of this can be attributed to the differences between the education and experience of service providers and their client groups. Kissane and Gingerich (2004) interviewed 51 directors from voluntary sector/ non-profit organisations operating in low-income neighbourhoods in Philadelphia in order to compare their views on the problems affecting the communities and those held by local residents. They found that the directors of these organisations emphasised the problems of unemployment and focused upon providing training and support for finding work. The top-five services identified by the service directors were job placement or job training, youth services, education, housing and health care. These priorities were not, however, shared by local residents, who were far more concerned with levels of violence and safety in their communities. Kissane and Gingerich (2004) suggest three possible explanations for the differences in views between voluntary sector directors and residents. The directors might acknowledge residents' views but feel that they are better placed to assess the problems and provide solutions. They could feel they meet the needs of residents whilst only representing a small cohort. Finally, it could be that the main problems and solutions change continually and are reflected at different times by residents and directors. This research could, however, also be used to show that the voluntary sector directors saw things from a relatively privileged position which prevented them from understanding the priorities of the communities they tried to serve. Although it could be argued that improving levels of employment in those communities could increase prosperity and help to reduce the problems of violence and crime, it is clear that these organisations were being run with priorities out of step with those of the community. By failing to understand the communities in which they work, workers in the voluntary sector severely limit the effectiveness of social intervention programmes. (see box 6b).

6b. Students on mismatch between community and organisation

Ann noted that the management team of the charity she worked for was dominated by people who were white and middle class, yet the bulk of the client group for this charity were working class and often from ethnic minority backgrounds. She claimed that this created a real problem, because those who directed the organisation had little understanding of their client group (Ann).

The social view of the community is useful as an explanation for the ways in which communities evolve to serve social needs. It can also act

learning about work

as a framework for those who are interested in social intervention and in responding not only to existing social needs but also to reassessing how these needs might change over time. Through recognising and supporting the connection between the welfare of the individual and the welfare of the community, social activists recognise where their responsibilities lie and draw attention to the symbiotic relationship between individuals and the community in the social campaigns they engineer. We have seen how the middle classes in particular are drawn to volunteering and how these activities rely upon people having sufficient economic stability to donate their time to others. We have taken a look at careers in teaching, social work, the police and the voluntary sector and have seen some of the benefits of immersing oneself in the community, though drawbacks have been identified when community involvement prevents professionals from fulfilling their primary functions. We need to be aware that when considering taking part in community activities, people often have to ask themselves to what extent they are happy with the existing character of the community. Professionals and volunteers need to consider the value they place on the existing culture of a community and be aware of the agendas of those who would seek to implant new cultural values. Community involvement could be viewed as an example of class-based cultural politics in which the poor and marginalised are subjected to the values and priorities of those from more affluent sections of society.

Social responsibility

It has been argued (see Taylor, Mellor and Walton, 2009) that higher education should help students to understand their role in the community and their responsibilities as citizens. This involves, amongst other things, illustrating the connection between individuals, the impact of the community upon the individual and identifying possible futures for the communities in question. By making use of work-related learning, students could develop different ways to understand their subjects and combine these with practical engagement in work. In so doing, students can become more aware of their own place and role in society and develop the confidence and skills necessary to participate in civic life. The Crick Report of 1998 (see Crick, 1998) called for citizenship education to develop the social and moral responsibility of students by encouraging them to recognise how their actions impact upon others and to think about the rights and responsibilities they have in the community. Work-related learning can be particularly beneficial. By asking students to consider how their experiences of work help them to understand their social and moral responsibilities, well-structured programmes of work-related learning can help students to assess their own place and role in society. It has been argued that work-related learning in the community is ' . . . more likely to develop altruism, philanthropy, self-reliance and personal social virtues than is a classroom-based, 'delivered' course of citizenship education' (Davison and Arthur, 2003, p. 21). In order to help students develop this understanding, it makes sense to focus upon some of the social and moral dimensions of work. By interacting with others, individuals enter into a series of relationships which could have a social and moral dimension. Regardless of the work they do, people should be able to consider the social and moral responsibilities they have as a result of their work. This can be illustrated by taking note of the experiences of workers in teaching, social work and the voluntary sector.

Teaching

Teachers can have a dramatic effect upon their pupils understanding of their rights and responsibilities as citizens. For example, citizenship education can help school pupils understand the importance of finding ways to integrate peacefully in a multicultural setting (see Starkey, 2007). In a comparative study of British and Hungarian teachers, Davies, Fulop, Hutchins, Ross and Berkics (2004) showed that teachers emphasise the importance of being a good person in the way they approach citizenship studies. Fairness, morality and responsibility towards one another were considered far more important than the more overt political dimensions of citizenship. Teachers in both countries believed that citizenship refers predominantly to human behaviour and to how individuals conduct themselves. Davies et al. also found that teachers in Britain were more likely than their Hungarian counterparts to talk about the importance of building and maintaining communities based upon mutual respect and clear values. There was a limit to which both groups of teachers looked outside of the individual. This was thought to create a real problem for those policymakers who support citizenship education in the belief that it can enrich the political culture and perhaps make their jobs a little easier. By focusing upon social and moral responsibility and by limiting the scope of citizenship education in this way, teachers might be guilty of downgrading the political features of citizenship. It should be evident that citizenship education in itself is not enough to convince people of their social responsibilities. Apart from anything else, the content of this citizenship education could be incompatible with the values of a particular community or group of people. Although teachers are in a position to promote particular views of social responsibility, this does not mean that their messages will be well received.

Social work

In a comparative study of social workers in the Netherlands and Estonia (see Sirotkina and van Ewijk, 2010) it was found that the way social workers view the responsibilities of citizens depends a great deal upon the existence or nonexistence of a welfare system in these countries. The Estonian state operates without an extensive welfare system and relies to a far greater extent upon family support. Because of this, social workers in Estonia subscribe to a narrow view of citizenship which concentrates mainly upon individual rights and assisting individuals to make the best of their lives. In the Netherlands, on the other hand, social workers operate within a mature welfare system in which their clients are viewed as citizens with responsibilities and '. . . as partners in the social care domain' (Sirotkina and van Ewijk, 2010, p. 82). Although social workers in Britain might support the idea of active citizenship and be active citizens themselves, the same does not necessarily apply to their client groups. According to Harris (2002), the rhetoric of active citizenship obscures a fundamental division between two types of citizen. The active citizens defended and promoted by politicians tend to be self-reliant, economically self-sustaining and able to dedicate some of their time to improving their communities. The recipients of social services and of unemployment benefits do not tend to fall in this category. Instead, they are often given rights as consumers of public services and perhaps encouraged to comment on the quality of the services they receive. These consumer-citizens do not tend to be active in the policy-making process or in the delivery of social services. We can see from the aforementioned research that social workers will often see their role as one of defending the rights of marginalised sections of the community. In order to do this, they will need to be able to find their way through the social and political system. Although they might be active citizens, their activities and commitment could, from a certain point of view, reduce the need for their client group to engage with the political process and thereby develop the skills necessary to become active citizens and embrace more fully their social responsibilities.

Voluntary sector

Those drawn to a career in the voluntary sector are often motivated by a sense of social responsibility. According to Cunningham (2012), the voluntary sector relies heavily upon the social and personal commitments of their workers. Research in the United States shows that attempts to motivate workers in the voluntary sector by linking pay and performance have backfired because making use of these private sector techniques have undermined their identification with the aims of the organisation. Cunningham also notes that 78% of voluntary sector workers in Australia were drawn to work for the voluntary sector because of their broader commitment to social change. For those surveyed, the voluntary sector provides workers with socially useful work and allows them to pursue their own social interests (Cunningham, 2012). The voluntary sector is also important in helping to empower local citizens. The lack of sustainable funding in the voluntary sector places limits upon what can be done and encourages voluntary sector workers to think in terms of how they can build the capacity of the local community rather than simply provide a service. Stuart Etherington (2006), for example, claimed that the failure of the state and private sectors to tackle inequality and long-term needs in the community created a need for the voluntary sector. These needs included problems of multi-generational unemployment as well as the problems associated with drug and alcohol abuse. He claimed that when governments turn away from such long-term and serious problems, people become more disconnected and alienated from their local communities and from the life of society. He believed that the voluntary sector was essential in the rebuilding of communities, encouraging active citizenship and in finding ways to create links between different sections of the local community. Politicians like David Blunkett (2001) claimed that citizens who have a stake in their communities respond differently in their behaviour to those who do not see themselves as integrated citizens. In his view, it is important to find ways to contribute to the community and to strengthen the bonds between neighbours. By participating in this way, individuals can enhance the lives of others as well as their own. If this is the case, it would appear that the way people understand their social and moral responsibilities can evolve through their participation in the community. It is not necessary for citizens to develop a philosophy of life based upon social and moral responsibilities prior to engaging in community projects. Indeed, it would appear that participation in itself can educate people in such matters.

Corporate social responsibility

Businesses in the private sector have also recognised their corporate social responsibilities through reinvesting some of their profits in community projects. Richard Branson (2008) claims it is essential that businesses recognise these broader social responsibilities. In his view, it is possible to make profits as well as contribute towards solving global problems. It was for this reason that he set up Virgin Unite, which looks into a range of international problems and looks for feasible solutions. He is convinced that '. . . capitalism – generously and humanely defined, and humbly working with others to understand the issues and solutions – can create some of those answers' (Branson, 2008, p. 289). Branson is aware of the responsibilities he has in the community and that his wealth and reputation can be used to promote the greater good and to intervene in political affairs. He claims that '. . . people in business and the very wealthy are in a unique position. They can connect with everyone, whether high or low, in any country, through a network of good will' (Branson, 2006, p.101). Branson is clearly now in a rather privileged position. Through his daring exploits, self-promotion and unde-niable business acumen, he is able to attract attention to a series of global problems and draw in leaders from business and politics to debate issues and provide funds and guidance. His insight into these problems does not necessarily stem from any first-hand experience of problems in his com-munity but would seem to owe rather more to his ability to step back from his role as an entrepreneur and apply his skills to dealing with his own list of worthy causes.

6c. Students on work and social responsibilities

Students have noted that being in employment can help to develop their sense of social responsibilities. Krissie's job as a cleaner in a large hospital meant that she often witnessed how vulnerable and afraid people can be and she claimed that '. . . working in the hospi-tal has partially inspired a sense of citizenship and community within me' (Krissie). Working in sales, Helen noted that some colleagues will attempt to force products on people regardless of their needs or ability to pay in an attempt to secure high commissions for themselves. She felt that it was important to recognise her social responsibilities and to take these into account when dealing with clients (Helen). It is not necessary to be at the cutting edge of community work to learn some-thing about social and moral responsibility. Indeed, some low-skilled work can bring people into contact with others and encourage them to think about their own behaviour and its possible impact on society.

When addressing the role of professionals and volunteers in advancing the benefits of social responsibility, it is also important for these groups to have a critical awareness of the values they promote and to see that enhancing social responsibilities does not necessarily do anything to reduce systemic problems. People might, for example, be encouraged to think that they have responsibilities for combating crime in their local area through involvement in neighbourhood watch groups or through participation in crime reduction partnerships. These organisations, however, deal with the problems of crime rather than the origins of crime. In themselves, they do not have the power or the remit to tackle some of the social origins of crime and thereby address the roots of the problem. Although it could be argued that this division between the problem and its origin cannot be bridged by community groups, it should also be evident that addressing the problem and ignoring the origin places considerable limits on what can be achieved. It could be, indeed, that the call for people to take on greater social responsibilities is made in the interest of keeping order and reducing the need for direct state involvement. By arguing that individuals have responsibilities within the community, the responsibility for social problems is dispersed through society as a whole. Although these groups are encouraged to ask questions about how to improve life within the community, these questions are formulated within relatively narrow terms of reference.

Conclusion

The concepts of social capital, community and social responsibility can be used to locate workers within a broader social context. Rather than see workers purely in terms of their attitudes towards their work or how they deal with their managers and colleagues, these concepts place workers within a rich fabric of social relationships and help to illustrate how many workers are influenced by their communities and in turn have some social impact. The concept of social capital furnishes a way to understand levels of trust in the community and to recognise that communities can block social interventions if they feel these initiatives are misguided, intrusive or of little use. Workers should recognise that they will sometimes need the support of the community and that the community might expect something in return. Workers can gain an insight into the social dynamics of their community and develop a real appreciation of its culture, pace and dominant characteristics. By gaining this understanding, workers can equip themselves with the skills necessary to intervene effectively and reflect upon their successes and failures. Community involvement provides not only knowledge of the community but also a conduit to effective intervention. This is particularly important for those professionals seeking to have a beneficial impact upon the life of the community and its members. These professionals can be particularly important in promoting social responsibilities within the community, partly through their own active citizenship but also through the messages they transmit and the negotiations they conduct with members of the community. Workers will be influenced by the communities in which they work and will in turn have the potential to develop social capital and promote the value of responsible citizenship. But workers need to be aware that they could be seen to be involved in social engineering. This could particularly be the case where there are stark contrasts between the social identities of the workers and the community. If workers are to have a beneficial impact in communities, it must start with developing an understanding of these communities. This can be facilitated by ensuring that members of the community are represented in the workforce, steering groups or consultative committees surrounding the professions.

Questions to consider

1. In what ways is social capital important in your relationship with colleagues at work?
2. To what extent is it important to understand the communities in which you work?
3. What social responsibilities do you feel you have?

A guide to reading

The theoretical foundations of social capital can be traced in Bourdieu (1986), Putnam (2000) and Fukuyama (1995). Arguments concerning its implications and influence in work can be seen in Russell (2014), Kuttner (1996) and Eadie (2001). Early theorists of community include Aristotle (1912 edition) and Rousseau (1968 edition). For a more recent study, see Beck (2000). Debates on the nature of citizenship and its relation to education can be found in Crick (1998). It is also possible to trace the importance of these concepts in different sectors of employment. For those interested in teaching, Ryan (2002) provides a useful introduction. The union perspective can be seen in Roach (2009), whilst Reed (2009) and Brooks (2009) provide reflective accounts. Literature on social work includes Ungar et al. (2004), Weil (1996), Harris (2002) and Sirotkina and van Ewijk (2010). For the police, it is worth looking at Terpstra (2009), Chappell (2009) and Yim and Schafer (2009). There are also plenty of sources on the voluntary sector, including Cunningham (2012), Lewin (2001), Span (2005) and Field (2005).

References

Alcock, P. (2000) 'Welfare policy'. In P. Dunleavy et al. (eds) *Developments in British Politics 6*, Macmillan: Houndmills, pp. 238–256.

Aristotle (1912) *Politic*, J. M. Dent: London.

Beck, U. (2000) *The Brave New World of Work*, Polity Press: Cambridge.

Bennett, R. (2001) 'Blair ditches pledges for challenges', *The Financial Times*, 11 January 2001, p. 1.

Blunkett, D. (2001) 'Volunteering: Volunteering is a means to active citizenship', *The Independent*, 9 October 2001, p. 4.

Bourdieu, P. (1986) 'The forms of capital'. In J.E. Richardson (ed) (1986) *Handbook of Theory of Research for the Sociology of Education*, Greenwood Press: New York, pp. 241–258.

Branson, R. (2006) *Screw It, Let's Do It: Lessons in Life*, Virgin Books/Random House: London.

Branson, R. (2008) *Business Stripped Bare*, Virgin Books: London.

Bridge, M. (2010) 'Laid off? Then start logging on', *The Times*, business section, 23 October 2010, p. 66.

Brooks, S.M. (2009) 'A case study of school-community alliances that rebuilt a community', *The School Community Journal*, Volume 19, Issue 2, pp. 59–80.

Chappell, A.T. (2009) 'The philosophical versus actual adoption of community policing', *Criminal Justice Review*, Volume 34, Issue 1, pp. 5–28.

Christie, F. (2005) 'Host organisations know they need to offer clear benefits in return for work', *The Independent*, 17 February 2005, p. 3.

Crick, B. (1998) *Education for Citizenship and the Teaching of Democracy in Schools: Final Report of the Advisory Group on Citizenship*, Qualifications and Curriculum Authority: London.

Cunningham, I. (2012) *Employment Relations in the Voluntary Sector*, Routledge: London.

Davies, I., Fulop, M., Hutchins, M., Ross, A. and Berkics, M. (2004) 'Citizenship and enterprise: Issues from an investigation of teachers' perceptions in England and Hungary', *Comparative Education*, Volume 40, Issue 3, pp. 363–384.

Davison, J. and Arthur, J. (2003) *Active citizenship and the development of social literacy: A case for experiential learning*, http://www.citized.info/pdf/commarticles/Arthur_Davison.pdf (last accessed 14 April 2008).

Eadie, A. (2001) 'It's a rum do, this rush for spirituality in the office', *The Daily Telegraph*, 26 July 2001, p. 68.

Etherington, S. (2006) 'Society: Charities: Careers: Comment: Time to seize the day – and make a difference', *The Guardian*, 15 February 2006, p. 4.

Field, J. (2003) *Social Capital*, Routledge: London and New York.

Fukuyama, F. (1995) *Trust: The Social Virtues and the Creation of Prosperity*, Free Press: New York.

Gold, P. (2000) 'The end of community?', *The Washington Times*, 11 June 2000, p. B8.

Gold, P. (2003) 'Junk food for the soul; relationship genre pushes social agenda,' *The Washington Times*, 9 September 2003, p. A19.

Halpern, D. (2005) *Social Capital*, Polity Press: Cambridge.

Harris, J. (2002) *The Social Work Business*, Routledge: London.

Jeffries, A. (1996) 'British conservatism: Individualism and gender' *Journal of Political Ideologies*, Volume 1, pp. 33–52.

Kissane, R.J. and Gingerich, J. (2004) 'Do you see what I see? Nonprofit and resident perceptions of urban neighbourhood problems', *Non-Profit and Voluntary Sector Quarterly*, Volume 33, Issue 2, pp. 311–333.

Kuttner, R. (1996) 'No market for civility', *The Washington Post*, 9 January 1996, p. A15.

Kymlicka, W. (2002) *Contemporary Political Philosophy*. Oxford University Press: Oxford.

Lewin, T. (2001) 'One state finds secret to strong civic bonds', *The New York Times*, 26 August 2001, p. 1.

Perry, M. (1993) *An Intellectual History of Modern Europe*, Houghton Mifflin: Boston.

Putnam, R. D. (2000) *Bowling Alone: The Collapse and Revival of American Community*, Simon and Schuster Paperbacks: New York.

Reed, W.A. (2009) 'The bridge is built: The role of local teachers in an urban elementary school', *The School Community Journal*, Volume 19, Issue 1, pp. 59–75.

Roach, P. (2009) *Speech to the Reach Out: Community Cohesion for Schools Conference*, NASUWT, 30 March 2009.

Rodger, J. (2000) *From a Welfare State to a Welfare Society*, Macmillan: Basingstoke.

Rousseau, J. J. (1968) *The Social Contract*, Penguin: Harmondsworth.

Russell, J. (2014) 'How to build trust at work', *The Washington Post*, 14 April 2014, p. A23.

Ryan, J. (2002) 'Promoting inclusive school-community relationships: Administrator strategies for empowering and enabling parents in diverse contexts, *Journal of Teaching and Learning*, Volume 2, pp. 1–20.

Sirotkina, R. and van Ewijk, H. (2010) 'Social professionals' perceptions of activating citizenship', *European Journal of Social Work*, Volume 13, Issue 1, pp. 73–90.

Snowdon, G., (2010) 'Work: 50 Steps to finding a new job', *The Guardian*, work section, 8 May 2010, p. 1.

Span, P. (2005) 'An exercise in community', *The New York Times*, 20 November 2005, p. 2.

Starkey, H. (2007) 'Citizenship education is about learning to live together and feeling part of a community', *The Times*, 23 January 2007, p. 3.

Taylor, G (2007) *Ideology and Welfare*, Palgrave: Basingstoke.

Taylor, G., Mellor, L. and Walton, L. (2009) 'Community involvement'. In M. McManus and G. Taylor, (eds) (2009) *Active Learning and Active Citizenship: Theoretical Frameworks*, The Higher Education Academy: Birmingham, pp. 132–149.

Terpstra, J. (2009) 'Community policing in practice: Ambitions and realisation', *Policing*, Volume 4, Issue 1, pp. 64–72.

Todd, M. and Taylor, G. (eds) (2004) *Democracy and Participation*, Merlin Press: London.

Ungar, M., Manuel, S., Mealey, S., Thomas, G. and Campbell, C. (2004) 'A study of community guides: Lessons for professionals practicing with and in communities', *Social Work*, Volume 49, Issue 4, pp. 550–561.

Warman, M. (2014) 'We "Mustn't smile too much", says cautious head of LinkedIn', *The Daily Telegraph*, business section, 23 June 2014, p. 5.

Weil, M.O. (1996) 'Community building: Building community practice', *Social Work*, Volume 41, Issue 5, pp. 481–499.

Yim, Y. and Schafer, B.D. (2009) 'Police and their perceived image: How community influence officers' job satisfaction', *Police Practice and Research*, Volume 10, Issue 1, pp. 17–29.

Learning through work
Skills development

chapter 7

Experiential Learning, Reflection and Communities of Practice

Work can teach people a great deal about who they are, their relations with others and their place in the wider community. The analysis presented so far in this book has attempted to show that the individual has opportunities to learn and to influence others at each level. We now turn to consider what individuals can do to develop their employability skills and to take more control over their own working lives. Learning from experience is necessarily different from traditional academic learning. Consider, for example, the difference between learning about the British parliamentary system from books, articles, the media and archives and learning about Parliament through working as an intern or as a research assistant for a member of Parliament. Whilst both forms of learning are important, they will reveal different things. Reflecting on the experience of work is one way to facilitate learning and to provide the individual with a foundation upon which to develop further. We start on this journey by considering the nature of experiential learning, its relationship to reflection and the value of participating in communities of practice.

Experiential learning

Experiential learning refers to the process by which people make sense of their experiences and translate them into concepts and thoughts. David

Kolb (1984) draws attention to a dynamic connection between learning and experience. He claims that people not only learn from experience but also gain understanding through building upon these experiences. He points out that '. . . knowledge is a transformation process, being continuously created and re-created, not an independent entity to be acquired or transmitted' (Kolb, 1984, p. 38). In his view, experiential learning helps to identify '. . . how experience is translated into concepts which in turn are used as guides in the choice of new experiences' (Kolb and Plovnick, 1974, p. 4). For Kolb (1984), ideas and concepts are not static creations but evolve over time as a result of experience. He believes that this helps to nourish our appreciation of the world and that '. . . our survival depends on our ability to adapt not only in the reactive sense of fitting into the physical and social worlds, but in the proactive sense of creating and shaping those worlds' (Kolb, 1984, p. 1). When attempting to come to terms with experiences, it is important to learn how to decipher the emotions these experiences generate. Beard and Wilson (2006) claim that experiential learning takes place on an emotional level, where the learner becomes aware of the emotions involved in an experience. It links experience and learning in a fundamental way and can be seen as a method used to incorporate experiences within the knowledge stored and as '. . . the sense making process of active engagement between the inner world of the person and the outer world of the environment' (Beard and Wilson, 2006, p. 19). Experiential learning, indeed, allows people to incorporate their emotions and experiences into the way they think and in turn interact with the world. Rather than see experiential learning as secondary to more traditional academic learning, it can be viewed as a synthesising method that helps individuals to combine their academic studies, their understanding of their own emotions and their evolving perception of their environment. Experiential learning might indeed be essential to anchor the individual and to at least encourage each person to consider the relative value of their intellectual, emotional and environmental awareness.

The experiential learning process

It becomes a lot easier to embrace the fundamentals of experiential learning once it is accepted that there is far more to education than learning a set curriculum. Rather than think solely in terms of accumulating knowledge on a particular subject, educators could provide students with intellectual challenges and adopt a more Socratic approach to teaching and learning in which the student is urged to consider problems rather than memorise solutions. This is deemed to be a particularly powerful force in human development (see Beard and Wilson, 2006). The learning process involves not only gaining access to new ideas but also learners reformulating the ideas they currently hold. Kolb (1984) talks about learning as being more akin to relearning and revising existing views rather than as a process that begins with a blank canvas. He points out that resistance within the learning process often takes place because people hold on to their old beliefs and try to protect these from scrutiny and revision. We have seen already (see chapter 5) that workers will sometimes resist changes at work if they feel these threaten deeply entrenched ways of approaching their jobs. It is important to realise, however, that knowledge is created and recreated over time. Kolb argues that to be effective learners, people need to access and develop four abilities. Firstly, they need *concrete experience*. Secondly, they need to be able to view these experiences from a variety of angles through *reflective observation*. Thirdly, they require the ability to formulate a conceptual awareness and develop a suitable theoretical framework through *abstract conceptualisation*. Finally, people need to make use of these theoretical frameworks to make decisions and to address and solve problems through what is referred to as *active experimentation*.

Kolb did not want these four abilities to be viewed as separate. Indeed, the experiential learning process involves these four feeding from one another. He recognised that the learner will often find ways to subordinate some abilities and to allow others to dominate. The relative balance of these abilities will be important in creating different forms of knowledge and in defining the way people see themselves. Whilst some people rely heavily upon their experiences, others will seek to strengthen their conceptual understanding of life. People who are reflective will be prone to view events in a variety of ways, whilst others will learn primarily from trying new things out (see Kolb, 1984; Kolb and Plovnick, 1974). By taking note of the four dimensions of the experiential learning process, it is possible to see more clearly some of the complexities involved in learning. Individuals might also be able to locate their own way of learning and identify how this differs from the methods used by other people. Being able to see this is particularly important when working in a team for, by revealing the preferences of each team member, it is possible to gain insight into the way different people work.

Kolb and learning styles

Kolb (1984) distinguishes between four main types of learners, who approach experience in different ways. The *convergers* are primarily cerebral and look for solutions to problems. The convergent learner is seen as somebody who prefers to deal with tasks that lend themselves to a single solution rather than deal with the complexities of social encounters. According to Kolb, they are often drawn to engineering, accountancy and medicine. The *divergers* tend to be imaginative and are able to consider the implications of what they observe. He claims that they are particularly good at mind mapping and are often at their best in settings involving the development of new ideas. These *divergers* are thought to be drawn to study subjects like history, politics, psychology and English and gravitate towards careers in education and social work. The *assimilators* are said to prefer to work with abstract theories and are apt to make use of theoretical models. This type of learner tends to be drawn to subjects like mathematics, economics and physics and to careers in management. Finally, *accommodators* are seen as being adaptable and considered able to apply ideas in a constructive and practical way. These people are thought to be particularly good at subjects like business and at careers in administration. According to Kolb and Plovnick (1974), people with a background in humanities and the social sciences seem to be able to approach concrete experiences in a variety of ways and to reflect upon these. They tend to be people with good imaginative abilities and those who work well in 'brainstorming' sessions. The divergent learning style captures this combination of abilities quite well.

Kolb, learning styles and career development

People often find that in order to advance in their careers, they need to find ways to integrate different learning styles into their basic pattern of work. Taking on managerial responsibilities, for example, will often rely upon developing the skills of an *accommodator* in which being able to identify practical solutions is particularly important (see Kolb, 1984). Kolb and Plovnick (1974) point out that interests people have will change over time and when these changes take place, they can find that their new interests come into conflict with the career path and attributes they have developed. People can also reach blockages in their careers and find that career progression relies upon the acquisition of new skills. According to Kolb and Plovnick (1974), individuals are influenced by different factors as they move through their careers. In the early stages of their careers, people are thought to be influenced primarily by issues of identity, which can lead to them choosing a career path without taking much note of their own learning styles. In the middle of their careers, people will be influenced less by the opinions of others and far more by their own need for fulfilment in work. If they attempt to change careers at this point, perhaps in the hope of finding more fulfilling work, these changes can be quite extreme and unsettling partly because of the way they impact on identity. Kolb and Plovnick (1974) argue that organisations need to take this into account because failure to do so can undermine the creative energy of their workers. These insights into stages in the development of careers illustrate the need to be able to adopt different learning styles. Although people might choose to enter a particular occupation because they believe it is consistent with the way they see themselves, it does not mean that they will have the right skills to thrive in this work and they might find it necessary to revisit the choices they made and find work that is more consistent with the way they think and learn. As people acquire new skills and attributes and as their self-perception changes, they might find it necessary to look for new challenges.

Critiques of Kolb

If we are to make use of the typology, we should do so with caution. Like any model, it is designed to draw attention to tendencies and to dominant characteristics rather than to say that all people will have characteristics drawn from one learning style to the exclusion of all others. Social scientists might make use of a divergent learning style, but this does not mean that they will be devoid of other skills and be unable to develop these abilities during their careers. Bergsteiner, Gaule and Neumann (2010) claim that there is ambiguity over whether Kolb's four learning styles are fixed categories or stages in the learning process. They argue that this is an important distinction because '. . . learning styles can be related to inherited or acquired personality types, while learning stages refer to sequential steps in the learning cycle' (Bergsteiner et al., 2010, p. 31). It could be argued, indeed, that Kolb's theory makes far more sense when these learning styles are seen as stages in the learning process rather than as fixed categories. Coffield, Moseley, Hall and Ecclestone (2004) point to the lack of empirical data to support the idea that individuals are predisposed to particular career choices based upon their learning styles. They criticise Kolb, moreover, for focusing far too much upon the individual and not enough upon the broader social and political context of learning. Rather than see learners as existing independently and without key social characteristics, they argue that individual learners are influenced by their class background, gender and ethnicity and that these should be factored into the way people are taught. It is clear, indeed, that the value of Kolb's conceptualisation of the learning process can be undermined by seeing each stage as a self-contained box within which to place individuals. Considerably more can be secured by recognising the importance of reflecting on experience, drawing connections with theoretical frameworks and making use of insights gained in decision making.

The idea of experiential learning can provide a useful framework to use when discussing the ways people learn through work. It challenges the view that all learning should take place by intellectually digesting a formal curriculum by showing the importance of processing experiences into useful and grounded knowledge. It shows how new knowledge is created through the conversion of experience into conceptual awareness and by providing individuals with a tool to use in their decision making. Experiential learning provides people with greater understanding of their own environments and a means by which they can process and make sense of the emotions generated by experience. We have made use of Kolb's ideas to illustrate key stages in the development of learning, whilst trying to avoid the problems of pigeonholing people into types of learners who never change. It is important to be aware that learning takes place within particular contexts and these contexts impact upon the value and transferability of the learning. We now move on to discuss the role of reflection in this process.

Reflection

There is far more to work-related learning than the accumulation of experiences. Many students graduate with relatively few years' experience of employment and can sometimes have difficulty in making the best of these experiences. This is where the art of reflection can be useful. Rather than simply describing what they have done, it allows for the deconstruction of these experiences and reveals to people what they have learnt from the process. Helyer (2010) points to the importance of using reflective powers to evaluate work and to improve performance. She claims that this involves '. . . looking both backwards and forwards (and sometimes sideways!) to make connections with what you are currently undertaking' (Helyer, 2010, p. 22). She refers to this process as a 'post modern approach to learning' (Helyer, 2010, p. 27) which enables the worker to reflect upon what is in the past, what is current and what could be. It is worth noting at this point that when people reflect, they do not simply take into account their most recent experiences. Indeed, they might consider new experiences within the context of prior experiences, their educational background and their assumptions about their own future. Individuals might sink into the past and revisit unresolved issues, especially if they have become disillusioned in their careers. On the other hand, they might be able to accommodate new experiences swiftly, especially if they are in jobs that are consistent with the way they think and feel about themselves. Reflection does not provide instant answers, but it can give people a tool to use in making decisions about work and in considering its value and its potential.

The importance of reflection

Through developing their reflective abilities, students might become more able to see the connections between their academic studies and their experience of work (see Stapleford, Beasley and Palmer, 2006). Effective learning can pull on what they learn in the abstract and what they learn from experience. As part of a more holistic approach to learning, making use of reflection can help individual learners develop an awareness of their own abilities and become more conscious of how they can combine different dimensions of their education. For example, a student working on a community project to raise awareness of the benefits of regular exercise would learn from the variety of people they encounter and would need to integrate this into their own understanding of the literature on the subject. To do this effectively, they would need to be able to draw comparisons between the theories they use and the practical experience of working in the community. They would also need to reflect upon their own health and approaches to exercise and perhaps access memories of how these messages had been communicated to them in the past and in the present. These students would therefore place themselves into a variety of settings and would effectively be surrounded by literature, their own experiences and the experiences of others. All of these might pull them in different directions and would need to be synthesised by the student reflecting upon the issues raised. This could in turn help the student become more autonomous. Hooker (2010) claims that the autonomous learner is somebody who is capable of directing his or her own learning and of making choices about the way they work and the things they learn. Whilst many learners begin by being quite dependent upon their teachers, autonomous learners are able to use their reflective powers to take control and to plan their own learning. This involves being able to formulate questions and devise new ways to study their subjects. New questions and approaches could be developed as a result of academic learning, experiential learning or through a combination of both.

Schon on reflecting in action and reflecting in practice

Reflection does not have to take place in retrospect but can be incorporated into the way people approach their work and make sense of this as an ongoing process. Schon provides a useful distinction between reflecting in action and reflecting in practice. Reflecting in action involves thinking about the activity whilst performing the action. This lies at the root of improvised practice and is an important feature of creativity. Reflecting in practice entails a person thinking about the patterns of behaviour so as to '... surface and criticise the tacit understandings that have grown up around the repetitive experiences of a specialised practice' (Schon, 1991, p. 61). According to Schon, the advantage of reflecting in action is that it allows for the development of new ways to approach practice through experimentation. He does recognise, however, that this approach to reflection could be seen as threatening to some professionals, especially if they regard their status as being tied to possessing a definite body of stable knowledge and understanding. It should be evident that reflection is used and advanced by those who embrace the ethos of continuing professional development. Reflecting in action in particular offers the possibility of a continual process of learning and one which situates the learner as a thinking and evolving being rather than as somebody functioning with a finite body of knowledge.

Ways to reflect

The ability to reflect is something that people can develop over time through engaging in the process. People might prefer to reflect using a template with set questions or through free-flowing writing exercises. According to Day (2010), making use of a learning log can be particularly useful in helping students to recognise the ways they make sense of their experiences over time. This learning log could contain a series of prompts to structure their reflections. Reflection could begin with a summary of key incidents and then move on to consider the feelings generated and assumptions about what others might feel about an incident. Alongside these emotional factors, a learner could also identify the skills used and their effectiveness. This learner might also place these experiences within an academic context containing relevant theories and concepts. Finally, learners might consider the implications for their own personal development and how they can enhance their abilities in the future (see Day, 2010). A learning log devised in this way would therefore summarise incidents, consider their emotional significance and place these within an academic and professional context. In each of these sections, however, it is important to recognise that the learner does not work in the present only but also pulls upon the past and speculates about the future.

7a. Students on the importance of reflection

Reflection does not come easily to all people. Stefanie claimed that she found reflection difficult, not only because it involved her being critical of her own abilities but also because, as a shy person, she was often reluctant to identify her own strengths. Over time, however, she had started to develop a more reflective approach to her academic and paid work, and she felt this had been important in her personal development (Stefanie). One student claimed that it '. . . allows you to assess situations and experiences in retrospect and decide whether you could have done something in a better way' (Helen). Jen described herself as '. . . an active learner who learns by doing and reflecting upon prior events and then taking what I have learnt forward to the next situation' (Jen). In each case, the students referred to reflection as something they do in retrospect as part of a planning process. It can help those who are shy and reluctant to promote their own abilities and those who prefer to learn by doing.

learning through work

The use of reflection in work-related learning

Reflection involves revealing connections between what has happened and drawing out the significance in theory and in practice. Students engaged in work-related learning need to be able to make sense of their experiences at work, consider how these experiences contribute towards the development of their own skills and employability and, ideally, make connections with some relevant literature from their discipline. Alderman and Milne (2005) point out that students need to be able to assess their own activities and monitor their own learning. They claim that this process of self-assessment '. . . can empower the individual and ensure learning experiences are more meaningful' (Alderman and Milne, 2005, p. 24). Gray, Cundell, Hay, O'Neil (2004) suggest that having the ability to reflect at work can help people to progress in their professional development. As we have seen, this learning often takes place outside of formal training. The skills people develop, moreover, will also be strengthened through engagement in a variety of activities. Gray et al. (2004) point out that communication skills can be developed '. . . through team meetings, in project work, in inducting staff into a new project, in presentations to line managers, and in effective use of email' (Gray et al., 2004, p. 176). Alderman and Milne (2005) claim that students can often suffer from a crisis of confidence when they begin their work-based learning. Sharing such concerns within a group environment can prove useful in helping students to understand and overcome problems they face. Moreover, such discussions allow students to revisit past experiences, unpack their emotions and evaluate their own learning.

It does not particularly matter whether the reflective process is conducted by individuals in isolation or within teams or support groups. In a comparative study of students studying social services and health and students of technology and transport (see Virtinan, Tynjala and Stenstrom, 2008), it was found that students were tutored in different ways in both their studies and in the work setting. Students in social services and health were tutored in the art of reflection and were generally more positive about their work-related learning than students studying technology and transport, who were given relatively little guidance on how to reflect. It has been argued that the reflective method used to teach in social services and health care helped these students to recognise their development and to take more control over their own work-related learning (see Virtinan et al., 2008). The important thing is that individuals draw connections between their experiences and look for ways to develop in the future. By reflecting upon their experiences at work, individuals will be able to monitor their own development and see their working lives as something they can manage and mould according to their interests. In this way, reflection can become empowering.

Making use of personal development portfolios

Personal development portfolios (PDPs) can be used by students to record their activities and plan for the future. These portfolios can include academic and nonacademic material and can be used by students to store valuable personal data, reflections and insights which can in turn be useful when applying for jobs. Students are advised to identify their skills and how they have developed these over time and to use their portfolios to set goals and develop action plans (see Edwards, 2005). Students are encouraged to think in terms of building e-portfolios of their work, which can then be used for presentations to employers. These e-portfolios could include written work, presentations, references from employers and reflective diaries in which students illustrated how they responded to key incidents. Employers have become particularly fond of this kind of evidence when interviewing for graduate-level employment (see Ward and Moser, 2008; JISC, 2009). The development of personal learning portfolios and e-portfolios of work might not capture the imagination of all students, but they can provide students with a portable record of their progress and can reveal to the keen critical eye some trends in their learning and some insight into who they are.

We should, however, be careful about attributing too great a value to reflection. Viewed in a positive light, it can provide people with a method used to take stock of their own development, make sense of their own past and perhaps provide some guidance on how to adapt their plans in response to changes in their own interests. Whilst educational developers and professional trainers might consider the ability to reflect as an essential skill in an ever-changing job market, there are clearly limitations to the reflective method. As a process, the value of what it produces depends a great deal upon what students place into the pot. To be effective, students must be willing to identify key incidents, access their emotional responses and draw connections between their insights and the theoretical underpinnings of their discipline. Learning logs and personal development portfolios will not necessarily attract the attention and support from all students. Traditional academic learning often involves studying 'the other' rather than reflecting upon oneself. This culture is deeply ingrained in the impersonal language used in academic writing and in discouraging students from talking in the first person in their assignments. If students and staff, especially in traditionally nonvocational subjects, are to make good use of the reflective process then this will almost certainly involve something of a cultural shift. In addition to making use of tools to assist in structuring their reflections, individuals can also learn from their colleagues. This learning can be deliberate and structured or it can flow from participating with others in a community of practice.

Communities of practice

A community of practice has been defined as '. . . a set of relations among persons, activity, and world, over time and in relation with other tangential and overlapping communities of practice' (Lave and Wenger, 1991, p. 98). Learning is thought to take place within these communities, which help to provide a framework and context for knowledge and a means by which people can participate actively in the learning process. These communities in turn evolve and change shape, depending upon the contribution of their members and the transformation of new members into experienced participants (see Lave and Wenger, 1991). Lave and Wenger (1991) argue in favour of decentred learning and making more effective use of communities of practice. Whereas traditional centred-learning involves the establishment of a hierarchical relationship between the master and apprentice, a decentred approach to learning recognises that those with knowledge should be embedded in a community of practice alongside other learners and that people learn as participants in these communities (Lave and Wenger, 1991). Communities of practice are particularly suited to a curriculum which places the learner rather than the teacher at the centre of the learning process and one that involves '. . . participation in an activity system about which participants share understandings concerning what they are doing and what that means in their lives and for their communities' (Lave and Wenger, 1991, p. 98). These communities are created by learners and can be particularly useful to aid in learning through work.

Importance of communities of practice for work-based learning

Individuals can learn through work within communities of practice. Fuller, Munro and Rainbird (2004) claim that by recognising the importance of communities of practice, attention can be diverted away from the individual having responsibility for his or her own learning, and it is possible to gain a greater appreciation of the collective nature of learning at work. Support is given to an expansive learning environment where individuals have the opportunity to participate in a variety of communities of practice and where workers are encouraged to develop their theoretical understandings of the work they do through participating in further training (see Fuller et al., 2004). The performance of individuals can be developed through participation in communities of practice as a result of the knowledge gained and the support provided (see Schenkel and Teigland, 2008). Communities of practice can benefit organisations because they can serve as a forum for sharing knowledge, experience, expertise and because they help to develop relationships in the workplace. They can also be important in embedding particular agendas in work. Moore (2007), for example, points to the pressure on workers in the National Health Service to keep abreast of new developments in policy and of changes in the organisation. In order to do so, they need to understand the importance of cultural diversity, issues around power and autonomy and be able to develop '. . . practical wisdom within supportive communities of practice' (Moore, 2007, p. 170). Communities of practice can also help to develop mechanisms for problem solving by providing a collective memory of tried and tested solutions. Through participating in the community of practice, individuals draw upon and contribute to the collective memory (Schenkel and Teigland, 2008). According to McArdle and Ackland (2007), organisations benefit because communities of practice provide opportunities for workers to dip in and out of different communities and to spread what they learn across an organisation. They believe that the new ideas generated in different communities of practice can help individuals to influence working practices and to forge stimulating relationships with their colleagues.

Communities of practice in teaching

According to Brouwer, Brekelmans, Nieuwenhuis and Simons (2012), the formation of communities of practice in teaching can have a positive impact upon the identity of teachers and their commitment to their vocation. In Brouwer et al.'s survey of secondary school teachers in the Netherlands, they revealed the importance of communities of practice for sharing expertise and resources and in helping to build a sense of community within the school. Researchers in teaching and learning in the higher education sector (see Gale, Turner and McKenzie, 2011) have also identified the benefits of lecturers participating in a community of practice. These communities are thought to provide lecturers with an opportunity to participate as learners and to help generate new understanding which can in turn influence their approach to teaching. In their view, research in teaching and learning can '. . . be a lived practice of constant becoming, based upon risk taking and disidentification, offering disruption, challenges to the habitual, and invitations into the unknown' (Gale et al., 2011, p.161). We can see that communities of practice can help to give professionals a sense of belonging, a forum for debate and a springboard for their own professional development.

Problems with communities of practice

Communities of practice are not necessarily suited to helping all participants reach their potential. In order to assess their value to their participants, it is important to recognise that these communities will be centres of power in their own right. Lave and Wenger have been criticised for paying too little attention to the importance of inequalities in power, for these inequalities impact upon the opportunities available to workers and barriers created to their learning (Fuller, Hodkinson, Hodkinson and Unwin, 2005). Rainbird, Munro and Holly (2004) claim that Lave and Wenger's analysis has limited applicability because it rests upon the relationship between teachers and learners in craft-based industries, it fails to give due weight to formal qualifications and it neglects to consider the insidious impact of power relations in limiting the scope and effectiveness of communities of practice. Indeed, groups will differ in the amount of power they have to protect themselves and this will stem from '. . . the extent to which their labour can be substituted by other workers; their ability to mount effective action and cause disruption; and their visibility' (Rainbird et al., 2004, p. 49). According to Fuller et al. (2004a), the participation of workers in learning is sometimes extremely limited and management can adopt a restrictive attitude towards the continuing development of their workforce. They point out, moreover, that learning at work is not necessarily beneficial for all workers because it can be used as a form of punishment, marginalise vulnerable sections of the workforce and lead to the intensification of work. Learning at work can thus be viewed as punitive, depending upon one's autonomy and place in structures of power.

It is also important to recognise the impact of experienced members to the character of a community of practice. Fuller et al. (2005) point out that Lave and Wenger failed to take into account the role of experienced workers, especially those who move into new work, because they concentrate too much upon the initiation of novices. This learning process is by no means one way, as experienced workers also learn from participating with new workers. Whereas Lave and Wenger tend to give the impression that workers gravitate towards the centre of communities of practice and reach a final destination, Fuller et al. (2005) argue that workers continue to learn through participating in these groups. They are also keen to show that new members of communities of practice exert considerable influence on the character of those communities by inputting their own life experiences, their experience of formal education and that this '. . . embodied person learns to belong in their new setting, adapting, developing and modifying their whole person in that process' (Fuller et al., 2005, p. 66). The critiques levelled against Lave and Wenger show that communities of practice should not be regarded as benevolent guilds in which masters pass on their skills to the novice, but they should be seen instead as constantly evolving networks which draw upon the energy and participation of workers connected by relations of power.

A community of practice can provide an interesting forum within which workers can cooperate, share knowledge and expertise, provide support to one another and initiate new arrivals into the culture of an organisation. These communities can be regarded as evolving frameworks designed to support learning and development. We have used examples from health care and teaching to show how communities of practice are important for helping workers keep abreast of policy changes in healthcare and to share innovations in methods of teaching. We have noted, however, that these communities of practice will tend to replicate inequalities in power. They are not necessarily open to all workers and can be used by management to provide opportunities for some workers whilst depriving others. Groups could be set up, for example, to fast-track certain individuals and to initiate these people into what is required for advancement. Communities of practice are not necessarily inclusive and can allow cliques to form with the support of management and to the detriment of those who find themselves excluded.

Conclusion

In making a case for experiential learning, we recognise its value as a supplement to traditional academic learning and suggest that integrating experience with academic concepts and theories can raise important questions and enrich the learning experience. It is argued herein that reflection provides learners with an important tool to record their experiences, process their feelings, make connections with their academic learning and plan their own development. Reflection can be used in a purely tactical way and dedicated to helping individuals make advances in their careers. It can also be used by people to consider how the various parts of their lives are connected and how work contributes or detracts from their quality of life. It is a tool that people can use at different stages in their lives and one that can help the individual make sense of his or her experience in a constructive way. It can empower people as learners, workers and as citizens. By reflecting upon key experiences, people are more able to look beyond the present and plan more realistically for the future. Some of this reflection might take place on an individual basis, but individuals also learn as part of groups. We have drawn attention to the importance of communities of practice to illustrate the value of collective forms of learning and to show that the individual is rarely in control of his or her own career development, but relies to a great extent upon working with others and to slotting into different groups within the work setting. We will need to take this into account as we move on to discuss some key work-related skills and how they contribute towards employability.

learning through work

Questions to consider

1. To what extent is it important to link your experience at work and the academic concepts used in your subject discipline?
2. Why does reflection allow you to draw connections between the past, present and future?
3. In what way does class, gender or ethnicity influence the way you learn?

A guide to reading

A foundation for experiential learning and reflection can be found in Kolb (1984). Beard and Wilson (2010) draw attention to the importance of understanding emotions. Bergsteiner et al. (2010) and Coffield et al. (1991) cast doubt on self-contained learning styles and remind the reader of the importance of the social context of learning. Schon (1991) is useful in showing the importance of reflecting whilst engaged in an activity. The role of reflection in work-related learning is covered by Alderman and Milne (2005), Gray et al. (2004), Virtinan et al. (2008) and Helyer (2010). For the theoretical foundations of communities of practice, see Lave and Wenger (1991). For a more critical approach to communities of practice, Fuller et al. (2004), Fuller et al. (2005) and Rainbird et al. (2004) are useful.

References

Alderman, B. and Milne, P. (2005) *A Model for Work-Based Learning*, The Scarecrow Press: Maryland.

Beard, C. and Wilson, J. (2006) *Experiential Learning: A Best Practice Handbook for Educators and Trainers*, Kogan Page: London.

Bergsteiner. H., Gaule, C. and Neumann, R. (2010) 'Kolb's experiential learning model: Critique from a modelling perspective', *Studies in Continuing Education*, Volume 32, Issue 1, pp. 29–46.

Brouwer, P., Brekelmans, M., Nieuwenhuis, L. and Simons, R. (2012) 'Communities of practice in the school workplace', *Journal of Educational Administration*, Volume 50, Issue 3, pp. 346–364.

Coffield, F., Moseley, D., Hall, E. and Ecclestone, K. (2004) *Should We Be Using Learning Styles?*, Learning & Skills Research Centre: London.

Day, H. (2010) *Work-Related Learning in English Studies: A Good Practice Guide*, The Higher Education Academy English Subject Centre: London.

Edwards, G. (2005) *Connecting PDP to employers needs and the world of work*, The Higher Education Academy: York.

Fuller, A., Munro, A. and Rainbird, H. (2004) 'Introduction and overview'. In Rainbird, H., Fuller, A. and Munro, A. (eds) (2004), *Workplace Learning in Context*. Routledge: London, pp. 1–18.

Fuller, A., Munro, A. and Rainbird, H. (2004a) 'Conclusion'. In Rainbird, H., Fuller, A. and Munro, A. (eds) (2004) *Workplace Learning in Context*, Routledge: London, pp. 299–306.

Fuller, A., Hodkinson, H., Hodkinson, P. and Unwin, L. (2005) 'Learning as peripheral participation in communities of practice: A reassessment of key concepts in workplace learning', *British Educational Research Journal*, Volume 31, Issue 1, pp. 49–68.

Gale, K., Turner, R. and McKenzie, L. (2011) 'Communities of praxis? Scholarship and practice styles of the HE and FE professional', *Journal of Vocational Education & Training*, Volume 63, Issue 2, pp. 159–169.

Gray, D., Cundell, S., Hay, D. and O'Neil, J. (2004) *Learning Through the Workplace: A Guide to Work-Based Learning*, Nelson Thornes: Cheltenham.

Helyer, R. (2010) 'Adapting to higher education: Academic skills'. In R. Helyer (ed) (2010) *The Work Based Learning Student Handbook*, Palgrave Macmillan: Basingstoke, 2010, pp. 10–62.

Hooker, E. (2010) 'Learning to learn: Practical advice for work based learners'. In R. Helyer (ed) (2010) *The Work Based Learning Student Handbook*, Palgrave Macmillan: Basingstoke, 2010, pp. 63–91.

JISC (2009) *e-Portfolios infoKit*, [online] Available from: http://www.jiscinfonet.ac.uk/infokits/e-portfolios [last accessed on 22 October 2010]

Kolb, D. (1984) *Experiential Learning: Experience As a Source of Learning and Development*, Prentice Hall: New Jersey.

Kolb, D. and Plovnick, M. (1974) 'The Experiential Learning Theory of Career Development', MIT Working Paper: Massachusetts Institute of Technology.

Lave, J. and Wenger, E. (1991) *Situated Learning: Legitimate Peripheral Participation*, Cambridge University Press: Cambridge.

McArdle, K. and Ackland, A. (2007) 'The demands of the double shift: Communities of practice in continuing professional development', *Journal of Vocational Education & Training*, Volume 59, Issue 1, pp. 107–120.

Moore, L. (2007) 'Ethical and organisational tensions for work-based learners', *Journal of Workplace Learning*, Volume 19, Issue 3, pp. 161–172.

Rainbird, H., Munro, A. and Holly, L. (2004) 'The employment relationship and workplace learning' in Rainbird, H., Fuller, A. and Munro, A. (eds) (2004) *Workplace Learning in Context*, Routledge: London, pp. 38–53.

Schenkel, A. and Teigland, R. (2008) 'Improved organisational performance through communities of practice', *Journal of Knowledge Management*, Volume 12, Issue 1, pp. 106–118.

Schon, D. (1991) *The Reflective Practitioner: How Professionals Think in Action*, Ashgate: London.

Stapleford, J., Beasley, L. and Palmer, S. (2006) 'Developing PDP to support employability: An institutional perspective'. In M. Yorke (ed.) *Personal Development Planning and Employability*, The Higher Education Academy: York.

Virtinan, A. Tynjala, P. and Stenstrom, M. (2008), 'Field specific educational practices as a source for students vocational identity formation'. In Billett, S., Harteis, C. and Etelapelto, A. (eds) (2008) *Emerging Perspectives of Workplace Learning*, Sense Publishers: Rotterdam, pp. 19–34.

Ward, C. and Moser, C. (2008) 'E-portfolios as a hiring tool: Do employers really care?' *Educause Quarterly*, Volume 4, pp. 13–14.

chapter 8

Leadership, Teamwork and Communication

As we move on to look at work-related skills, our focus will be upon a series of generic skills that are used across sectors. We look in particular at the skills necessary to work with other people in a professional setting. These include the ability to take the lead, to work in teams and to communicate effectively. When we join a team, we need to take into account its distinctive character and ethos. People will assume different roles within teams and their contribution will depend upon the skills they have and the degree of autonomy they secure over their own work. In this chapter, we will take a look at the way teams work and the roots of conflict in teams. When working within teams, it is essential to develop suitable communication skills. These will vary across sectors and will change at different levels of the socio-economic system. We need to examine the nature of communication, the value of different types of communication and discuss the implications of poor communication. In looking at teamwork and communication, we will be concerned primarily with identifying how improvements can be made, in the belief that it furnishes the individual with key transferable skills and can contribute significantly to the fulfilment people feel in work. In addition to outlining the skills and illustrating how these skills could be developed, examples will be used from key sectors of employment to show how these skills are applied in the work setting.

Leadership

It has been noted that a leader is somebody who '. . . sets the tone by starting the conversations, asking the important questions, and making sure the right people are in the room at the right time' (Berkun, 2008, p. 60). Leadership can also be seen as '. . . an invisible force that guides the team' (Mersino, 2007, p. 191). Leaders do not only make decisions and provide solutions, they also need to identify priorities and ask pertinent questions. Building upon extensive work with 2,500 directors and managers in the United States and in Western Europe, Williams (2005) drew attention to a number of individual attributes and social skills needed for leaders to be effective. The individual attributes needed by leaders include being able to identify clear goals, understand how to influence the broader perspectives of an organisation, to work with integrity and the ability to solve problems by looking beyond immediate problems and obstacles. Good leaders also need to work well with their teams and have the emotional intelligence necessary to judge what should be communicated, how best to do this, the ability to build and sustain strong relationships and to galvanise the creative energy of their colleagues. In what follows, we will take a look at some of these key leadership qualities.

Leadership and the ability to inspire

Management consultants point to the inspirational qualities of good leaders. The ability to inspire might surface through helping to articulate a vision for an organisation or particular project or through being able to '. . . make work attractive and interesting to the team, create high team morale, and attract and retain good resources' (Mersino, 2007, p. 174). Some people are able to lead because of the sheer force of their personality and the depth of their passions. Consider, for example, the dynamic leadership of Bob Geldof in setting up the Band Aid and Live Aid projects during the 1980s. Band Aid involved the recording of a single by a collection of successful musicians to raise money to relieve suffering caused by the famine in Ethiopia. The commercial success of this single prompted Geldof to arrange Live Aid in London and Philadelphia. Geldof was able to inspire musicians to cooperate and to give their time to the cause and in so doing helped to capture the imagination of the world (see Hillmore, 1985). Other people attempt to inspire through innovation. Richard Branson (2008), for example, is very critical of dictatorial methods of leadership. For him, it is important to reflect upon your own strengths and weaknesses and to assemble teams to share skills and to work together in an effective way. He described himself as an entrepreneur rather than as a manager. In Branson's view, his role is to develop new ventures and to seek out opportunities rather than to run any of his businesses. It is evident that he gains a thrill from uncertainty and potential and that, once a business is established, he has relatively little interest in the day-to-day delivery of a product or service. He claimed, indeed, that the '. . . entrepreneur's job is effectively to put themselves out of a job each time the new company is up and running' (Branson, 2008, p. 260). This ability to inspire is considered an important part of leadership. The examples outlined earlier show how it can be applied on a grand scale, but the ability itself is equally as important for small teams and modest ventures.

8a. Students on leadership, vision and strength

Students suggest that leaders need the ability to inspire. Talking about his role in a project for an external organisation, Alistair said that he had to '. . . make sure that I was always enthusiastic and show them that I believed in the project and that it would work' (Alistair). Tasha felt that leadership '. . . emerges as someone expresses such confident commitment to a project that others want to share in their optimistic expectations' (Tasha). For these students, leaders need confidence in their own abilities. They believe that the ability to inspire derives from this confidence.

Building trust

In order to be effective, leaders need to be able to convince their teams that they can be trusted. This does not necessarily involve promoting their own virtues to the team, but can be approached by attempting to build a culture of trust within the team. Berkun (2008) suggests that the key to leadership is to keep things simple and practical. He claims that leaders should take responsibility, consult when necessary and be ready to make difficult decisions. The way teams respond to such decisions will often depend upon the level of trust and confidence they have in their leader. This is clearly something that can be developed and matured over time. Lock (2007) points out that people generally appreciate being led by somebody who '. . . displays competence, makes clear decisions, gives precise, achievable instructions, delegates well, listens to and accepts sound advice, is enthusiastic and confident, and thus generally commands respect by example and qualities of leadership' (Lock, 2007, p. 156). In order to build trust, leaders must be aware of the values and internal dynamics of their teams and be able to work effectively within their own work culture.

Understanding broader contexts

Leaders need to consider not only their own personal strengths, their abilities to inspire and how to bring out the best in their teams but also the broader contexts within which they work. Management consultants point to the importance of knowing the rules of the game in any particular industry and in constructing a career plan which takes these rules into account. Richard Templar advises people to '. . . study your chosen industry and see the progression steps needed to make it to the position you want to occupy' (Templar, 2003, p. 46). Leaders will often need to work across different cultures and adapt their skills to different cultural contexts. As part of this, it is important to be '. . . tuned into information gathering and analyses in order to uncover hidden cultural assumptions and become aware of how culture is shaping perceptions' (Engelbrecht, 2012, p. 158). When discussing the importance of work for identity (see chapter 2), we saw how each organisation will also have its own values and that understanding these values can help workers to adjust to the demands of their employers and to the rhythms of working with their colleagues. This is also the case for those who take on leadership roles, as they will often find that they need to mediate between the needs of the organisation and those of the staff.

Changing over time

The demands placed upon people at work will change and the way they respond to these demands will depend upon the way they reflect upon their experiences. Leaders will change because of what they encounter in their roles. Consider, for example, the way in which Tony Blair adapted to his role as prime minister. Blair (2010) was aware that he was a different type of Labour leader, partly because he had a middle-class background and because he embraced aspirational values. He admitted that he had very little time for those who spoke of class warfare and wanted instead to find ways to unify the nation. He recalled that during his time as prime minister, his leadership style changed dramatically. When he entered office, he believed he possessed a real feel for what the electorate wanted. So much so that he was considered '. . . one who could express the public's thoughts and therefore shape them, the one who would sniff the scent of popular opinion and follow it with a certain intuition' (Blair, 2010, p. 602). By the time it came for Blair to leave office, he felt that he had lost this ability. He talked about evolving into a different type of leader who would '. . . do what I intuitively thought right, not what I intuitively guessed was popular' (Blair, 2010, p. 603). He claimed that he was no longer interested in responding to the popular will and that he had started to see leadership '. . . not as knowing what people wanted and trying to satisfy them, but knowing what I thought was in their best interests and trying to do it' (Blair, 2010, p. 661). By adopting this change in leadership style, Blair became more divorced from diverse opinions within his own party and within the electorate. This was by no means an accident. It would appear that Blair made the decision to prioritise his own views above pressure from the public and from the ranks within the Labour Party. In so doing, he became a different type of leader.

Leadership in social work and health care

The type of leadership skills required will vary between sectors and will no doubt change with the evolving culture of each profession. When directors of social work programmes in the United States were asked to define what makes a good leader, they claimed that they must be committed to ethical behaviour, inclusive decision making and altruism (see Fisher, 2009). In many professions, leaders will find that they have to work across sectors and be willing to adapt to a range of diverse occupational cultures. According to Gau and Company (2007), the role of social workers in American hospitals has been transformed because of market pressures within the health service. Under these conditions, social workers have had to adopt a strategic vision of how social work can dovetail with the provision of health care. This has involved developing important networks within hospitals and in the broader community. Because of this, leaders within social work departments are expected to have a clear understanding of the policy context, of how to respond rapidly to changes in funding and priorities and to involve colleagues in important decisions about how to position social work within hospitals. The importance of multiagency work can also be seen in the changing role of healthcare leaders in South Africa (see Ansari, 2009), who are increasingly expected to work with a range of stakeholders from the public, private and third sectors. These leaders have found that it is important to understand and be able to work with groups holding different degrees of influence and organised according to different models of power. The skills required by these leaders include having an understanding of the internal workings of each group, how to collaborate and communicate effectively with different groups. It should be apparent that working with different groups will exert extra pressure upon leaders, who need to operate not only in accordance with their own occupational culture but also respond to the culture and methods used by their allied professions and partners.

Effective leaders are those who can look beyond mundane tasks and develop a strategic vision which can be communicated to others and give a sense of direction to their enterprise. Successful leaders are those who are able to build trust, work across different organisational cultures and gain the cooperation of others. They are those who are able not only to respond to the dominant occupational cultures but also shape them through taking on board both the internal dynamics of teams and the pressure exerted by external groups and hierarchies. It would be wrong to assume, however, that all dimensions of leadership can be taught. Whilst it is possible to guide people to understand strategic drivers and to highlight some of the personal characteristics needed by leaders, good leadership relies upon the existence or cultivation of emotional intelligence. Without this, leaders will be unable to understand the needs of their teams. Whilst they might be able to introduce strategies to secure cooperation and compliance, they will be unable to secure the trust and confidence of other workers in the team.

Teamwork

Teams differ from a random collection of individuals by having a collective sense of identity. Belbin (2010) referred to a team as '. . . a set of players who have a reciprocal part to play, and who are dynamically engaged with one another' (Belbin, 2010, p. 98). Individuals within teams will have expectations placed upon them and will in turn expect things from their colleagues. Managers might choose to meet with colleagues to discuss and define roles in the team, identify the responsibilities of each member of the team and highlight where these responsibilities are shared. This would serve to establish the expectations and assumptions of team members, to show where there is agreement and, conversely, where problems could arise. The exercise outlined earlier provides a framework which enables individuals to discuss their roles and responsibilities openly (see Berkun, 2008). It takes time for individuals to find their place within a team and to see themselves as developing alongside others. Being accepted in a team can have a positive impact upon the way people view work, whilst being ignored or rejected by a team is liable to contribute towards feelings of isolation and alienation. Teams can help to provide workers with support and can be particularly important in reducing boredom at work, especially where the work involves performing repetitive tasks (see West, 2012). When joining a team, individuals need to focus upon their own roles, the collective functions and purpose of the team and the team's distinctive character, personality and rhythm. If they can do this, they will become a lot clearer about their own place within the team.

Forming teams

Teams are sometimes created to perform a particular function. A team might be created as a short-term measure or with an eye to greater longevity. It might be formed, for example, to develop a product. It could begin as a group of strangers, who have been selected because of their experience in product design. As soon as the product design has been finalised, the team could then be disbanded. At this point, another team could take over to turn this design into the final product. Hind and Moss (2011) claim that newly formed teams will tend to go through four stages in their development. They used the terms *forming, storming, norming* and *performing* to describe these stages. In the *forming* stage, individuals group together to share ideas and to discuss approaches to the task at hand. The *storming* stage tends to involve arguments over how to distribute power and responsibilities within the team. In the *norming* stage, most of these disagreements have been resolved and the team attains some stability. In the final stage, teams are able to concentrate far more upon *performing* their tasks. From the stages outlined here, it is apparent that teams will need to go through periods of instability before they are able to perform their primary functions. They will need to find ways to facilitate communication, promote a shared understanding of the purpose of the team and will have to endure conflict as different interests emerge. Although the logic of this sequence would tend to suggest that this instability is required before a team finds it can function smoothly, it is also the case that teams will sometimes become locked into internal arguments and will find it difficult to make the transition from the *storming* stage of development. We have seen already (see chapter 5), that cultures of resistance can develop in teams in response to management attempts to implement change. A new team developed in this volatile climate may well find that the barriers to effective working together rest not only on the internal dynamics and personality mix of team members but also on attitudes towards the changes proposed. It is quite conceivable that deep divisions will emerge and make it difficult for the team to function smoothly.

The importance of teamwork

In an interview situation, interviewers often look for people who can make a significant contribution to a team. This contribution extends beyond the performance of mere tasks. People are judged according to whether they will fit in and whether they can bring some new energy to the team. Melton (2003) claims that those interested in professional work need to be able to collaborate with others. He notes that in Western culture, this often relies upon getting people to commit to playing a definite role and a willingness to work collectively on identifying problems and developing solutions. This model of teamwork cannot be applied universally, as some non-Western cultures seem less willing to accept the overt questioning of team members and the collective examination of weaknesses. Whilst teams are not necessarily democratic, they often require team members to commit to participate in the development of collective endeavours.

Templar (2003) claims that it is important for people to understand their particular roles within their teams. Although teams might primarily be concerned with developing ideas, they also require people to implement these ideas. It is worth remembering that teams do not necessarily function automatically and that some team members might need to dedicate their time to coordinating others (see Templar, 2003). Richard Branson (2008) pointed out that teams need to change over time in order to maintain creativity and energy. Those who manage teams, according to Branson, need a reasonable amount of emotional intelligence to bring out the best in a team. Work-based learning offers individuals the opportunity to develop their interpersonal skills and increase their appreciation of team dynamics. An individual can learn to function as a team member, to assist others in a team through reflecting upon the skills they have and comparing these skills to those of other team members (see Raelin, 2008). According to this line of reasoning, which concentrates upon the creative potential of teams, it is important to look beyond what individuals can contribute to a team and to focus upon how teams work together and how the creative energies of teams evolve over time. Individuals are not merely passive members of teams but can also influence their character and development. We saw when discussing communities of practice (see chapter 7), the importance of cross-fertilisation between teams and how individuals should not be viewed as locked within a single team which defines their approach to work. Instead, individuals adapt to different cultures and take the influence of these cultures into the different teams within which they work.

Belbin on the character and development of teams

Belbin (2010) argues that strong and well balanced teams will make use of individual differences and will recognise the need for different roles within a team. Some people will be *shapers*, who specialise in inspiring others. *Coordinators* will understand the importance of drawing upon diverse skills within the team. *Implementers* will have a practical approach to getting the work done, whilst *completers* will be needed to assure the quality of the final product or service. He claims that building a successful team must start by establishing what each person has to offer and 'casting' people according to their strengths. In Belbin's view, problems occur within teams when individuals are miscast or are expected to carry out functions inconsistent with their own dominant traits and strengths. It is evident that sometimes individuals are unable to work well in a particular team and that teams will not work well if they are overloaded with shapers, coordinators, implementers or completers, although all of these roles are important and should feature in a team.

Teams are not meant to be permanent structures. They will develop to deal with particular tasks and will continue for as long as those tasks need to be completed. The character of the team will, however, change over time. This does not mean that the team necessarily gets any better or becomes more efficient. Changes in personnel and the suitability of different styles of management will have an impact. Belbin (2010) illustrates this by tracing the development of a fictional team. He shows that a consultative culture might develop in reaction to the failure of a team organised along authoritarian lines. This new era of consultation, however, will tend over time to breed conformity as people become reluctant to be overtly critical of the new management. Under these conditions, problems will remain unreported and the team will become complacent. If this in turn leads to failure, the circumstances are created for the rise of a new authoritarian culture. We see in this a circular pattern. Understanding this pattern can assist in tracing the development of teams and their authoritarian or consultative ethos and might even help managers to avoid pushing the team to one of these extremes and to focus instead upon what is sustainable. As authoritarian and overly consultative teams would appear to be flawed, a case could be made for a blended approach in which consultation takes place and clear lines of authority are understood. This view of the potential of teams to exist without overt conflict and to function in the interests of the whole does, however, fail to take into account the existence of systemic inequalities and how these can contribute towards alienation, resentment and resistance (see chapters 3–5). Teams do not exist in a sociopolitical vacuum and might not be amenable to the rational and compliant patterns of work favoured by management consultants.

We should note that models designed to maximise the efficiency of teams should be applied with care. Those who are involved in providing management training have a vested interest in promoting a transferrable model which can apply in a variety of settings. Participants in this form of training are asked to consider the value of the models put before them and to use these as frameworks to assess their own experiences of work. Although it might be tempting to regard these models as tried and tested, it is clear that they are constructed from a management perspective in which workers need to be herded, cajoled and managed within firm boundaries. Whilst this form of management structure might be common in corporations, it does not necessarily suit all organisations. Small third sector cooperatives, for example, would understandably be resistant to the management formula outlined earlier.

Conflict in teams

Although conflicting ideas and perspectives can sometimes be creative, interpersonal conflict can be disruptive and divert the attention of team members away from their work. Billingham (2008) insists that combining people with different characteristics in demanding situations invariably leads to conflict. Whilst little would need to be done about small disagreements, some conflicts may require skilful negotiation and diplomacy on the part of management. Conflict can stem from clashes in personality, differences in age and outlook, hidden agendas and arguments over the allocation of resources. Depending on the situation, managers might choose to ignore differences, find ways to accommodate differences or look for ways to compromise (see Billingham, 2008). Conflicts can arise when people fail to pull their weight in a team. Viewed from a project management perspective, Spolander and Martin (2012) claim that the free-rider is often allowed to get away with contributing little, partly as a result of his or her own abilities but also because of the compliance of the group. The free-rider will find ways to pass on responsibility to other people in the group. This can sometimes go undetected, or at least unchallenged, and can occur when teams focus upon outputs rather than on the way they work collectively. Members of a team might even cover for the free-rider so as to minimise the prospects of micromanagement techniques being imposed upon the team as a whole. Concealing the shortcomings of a team member might be necessary to maintain the illusion of a well-structured and efficient team. We should note, however, that the approaches outlined earlier demonise those who resist in teams by proceeding from the assumption that teams should work if they are constructed sensibly. These approaches do not provide room for individuals who swim against the tide not because they have problems with teamwork itself but because they object to what a team is attempting to do.

Teamwork in social work and teaching

Social workers often work as part of multidisciplinary teams, where different groups will have had different training and be exposed to divergent work cultures. Howe, Hyer, Mellor and Lindeman (2001) claim that the training of social workers should include gaining an insight into these different cultures so as to ease the way for multidisciplinary teams to work together. Training packages, such as those developed by the John Hartford Foundation, involved teamwork and exposed trainees to the roles and working practices of allied professions. The use of peer support through teams has become an important part of the work culture for teachers. These teams have been created to share resources, provide mentoring and a safe space to scrutinise practice and engage in collective problem solving (see Ohlsson, 2013). We can see that teamwork can be integrated into the formal curriculum of those training for the professions and be reinforced through engaging in communities of practice and taking advantage of opportunities for collective reflection. In professions where teamwork is essential, management might take active steps to encourage teams to develop strategies to work more efficiently and acquaint their teams with the values held, and methods used, by key stakeholders.

Teams are not merely created for administrative convenience or to ease the management of individuals. They often have a particular function and this will be one of the factors contributing towards their character. Individuals might be members of multiple teams simultaneously, as work is divided into different tasks. A good case could be made for individuals understanding their own roles within teams, the dominant characteristics of their teams and how they differ from allied teams and key stakeholders. Although teams can assist individuals at work, they can also be a source of stress and the site of conflict. Managers clearly have a vested interest in finding ways to alleviate conflict and to make these teams work more effectively in the interest of the organisation. We should recognise, however, that teams are often built with contradictory aims. On the one hand they seek to define and prescribe the roles of each individual within a team and can thus be seen as limiting, whilst on the other hand seek to make use of their collective energy. There is no reason to believe that individuals will be committed to both performing their individual functions and to enhancing the performance of their teams. Too many other sociopolitical factors can intrude and derail the team-building exercises favoured by management. As we will see, problems can arise in teams because of flaws in the communication methods used.

Communication

Communication is not concerned solely with the transmission of information. Chan (2002) points out that real communication takes place when somebody sends a message that is received and understood by the recipient. If the message is not understood, then real communication has not taken place. According to Chan, good communicators will have a reasonable insight into the attitudes and dispositions of their audience and will be clear about what they want to say. Chan argues, moreover, that listening skills can be improved if people consider and reflect upon why they want to know what is being communicated and take note of how they listen (see Chan, 2002). Rather than see communication as a one-way process, benefits can accrue from factoring in perceptions of the audience and observing the methods used to listen and respond to others. It should be clear that the way people communicate can produce an emotional response which might help or hinder good working relations. Mersino (2007) recommends using a considered approach when communicating, which takes into account a person's own emotions, the emotions of others and their possible reactions. This will no doubt involve a fair amount of guesswork. Even if people are aware enough to capture the fundamentals of their own emotions, they still need to be able to empathise with others and be able to identify possible emotional reactions.

8d. Students on developing communication skills

Working on a group project in a local secondary school, Ria said that the group rehearsed before their meetings with the school and reflected as a group upon the success of these meetings. These reflections were then captured in a brief written record, which was distributed to all team members and shared with the school. Jackie recalled that the experience of working in a school had improved her non-verbal communication skills. She found that she had to fight against her natural shyness, and she claimed that she became aware that her 'posture

---

and demeanour' had improved as a result of her work (Jackie). For these students, working in the school had challenged their communication skills because of having to liaise with the management of the school and find ways to connect with the school pupils. In some ways, they felt as if they were being pulled in different directions, but they recognised the importance of developing their communication skills and approaching their work in a professional manner.

Working in the hospitality industry, Kate recalled that she had to practise her communication skills and attempt to conceal her nerves in preparation for her work with demanding and intimidating clients. She claimed that this was essential because of her shy demeanour. She found working on her body language was particularly important in helping her to project greater levels of confidence (Kate). Molly noted that her communication skills were developing continually as a result of her part-time work in the retail sector, her work on group projects at university and through her training as an appropriate adult for the Youth Justice Service (Molly). These students noted that their communication skills go far beyond the way they speak and are developed continually in a variety of settings. They also recognise the value of reflecting upon the ways in which their communication skills were developing.

The importance of clarity

In order to communicate well, it is necessary to be clear about the message you want to release. Richard Branson (2008) claimed that good communication often relies upon being concise and disciplined about what is communicated. He warned against spending too much time on phone calls and emails because he felt it often reduced the time available for more creative endeavours. In order to maintain the integrity of the *Virgin* brand, Branson talked about the importance of being clear about what *Virgin* can offer and its place in the market. Alex Ferguson (2013), the former manager of Manchester United, knew that he needed well-developed communication skills to handle the demands of the media and to protect his players from unfair criticism. He recalled that it was essential to prepare himself before meeting the media and that, over time, he learnt how to read the subtext of their questions and gain an appreciation of their motives. With an unshakeable commitment to protecting his players and keeping a firm eye on the next game, Ferguson resisted the temptation to entertain the media and concentrated instead upon providing a coherent and consistent message about the abilities of his players and the character of Manchester United. Branson and Ferguson note that effective communication must be rooted in having something clear and precise to say. They realise that although they will not always be in control of the agenda of meetings, especially when this involves facing a probing media, they need to craft their messages and reaffirm their core values in what they choose to share with others.

The problem of poor communication

Berkun (2008) suggests that some of the most common communication problems include making assumptions about what is being said without seeking further clarification, failing to listen carefully, neglecting to provide explanations for decisions made and engaging in personal attacks. In Berkun's view, team members should be encouraged to identify problems as they arise, whilst team leaders are urged to consider their own behaviour and to reflect upon what they say and how they say it. According to Beamish (2008), communication problems occur because of the behaviour of those who transmit information and those who receive it. It might, for example, be unclear who requires information. Those who have a message to transmit might fail to do so if they lack confidence in the value of what they have to say. Problems can also occur when those who receive messages regard them as too negative or threatening. It would appear that good communication requires not only the ability to craft a clear message but also ensure that the message crafted is relevant to the audience and stated in a way to minimise resistance. This is not about making messages bland and unchallenging but about considering the purpose of communication. For example, people might make a small contribution to a debate in a meeting or want to say rather more as part of an attempt to convince others of a certain point of view or perspective on a problem. Meetings might be spent looking for common ground between opposing factions within a team in the hope of helping to devise a consensus. Each of these approaches to a meeting will call upon people to use different ways to communicate. Although each of the examples given relies upon listening as well as talking, there will still be a need to make rather more use of emotional intelligence if the intention is to build a consensus rather than simply to add a comment or piece of information to a debate.

8e. Students on the importance of communication

Chloe noted the importance of active listening in her communication with colleagues and clients. She recognised that her communication skills consisted not only in what she said but also in her non-verbal communication. She saw the importance of maintaining eye contact, mirroring facial expressions and adjusting the physical space between herself and others in an appropriate way (Chloe). Mark claimed that he had developed a 'new found respect and understanding' for good communication skills and had discovered that '. . . empathy and understanding

learning through work

was needed, on both sides, in order to prevent small issues becoming more problematic' (Mark). Developing good communication skills does not necessarily entail focusing only upon what is transmitted. Harlan was aware that he needed to be more restrained in a group setting. Describing himself as a 'bit of a chatter box', he realised he needed to allow more room for other members of the group to contribute to discussions and gain more confidence in their own ideas (Harlan). Students have found that taking on positions of responsibility can improve their confidence. One student recalled that '. . . I can be shy around new people and can sometimes take longer to come out of my shell than others, but having the opportunity to manage other people . . . really allowed not only my leadership but also my communication skills to flourish' (Brooke).

Understanding others

The uncertainty created at work by poor communication can be reduced to some extent by developing an awareness of what is said, how to listen and ways to decipher what others have to say. According to Bjerlov and Docherty (2006), people could begin by drawing a distinction between their own views and the views held by others. People might also subject their own views to scrutiny as a precursor to shifting their views. In the context of a meeting, people might differentiate between their own views and those of their colleagues, especially if there is a discernible rift between the views being expressed. Once this has taken place, they might choose to dig in and to continue to argue their case regardless of opposition. By shifting their own position to make their key priorities more palatable to those who hold opposing views, they might find ways to forge an agreement in the meeting. This might mean abandoning some of the more marginal features of their argument and blending these with opposing ideas.

It is always important to consider the cultural values of an audience when attempting to communicate, especially if the intention is to convince or convert that audience to your own view. Tony Blair (2010) provides an interesting story about what can go wrong when you fail to take into account the existing values of the audience. He recalled that he had prepared a speech on the criminal justice system and made the mistake of presenting it to a gathering of the Women's Institute. Although he felt his speech was well written and argued clearly, he soon became aware that his audience were far from receptive. This became abundantly clear when they greeted his speech with a slow handclap. In retrospect, he realised that the tone of the speech was far more suited to a group of professors than to the audience he had selected. It is evident that Blair had concentrated far too much on the transmission of his message and not enough upon how this message would be received. It is important to realise that this event could be interpreted differently. Whilst Blair was convinced that his speech was well written and well-presented and that he had simply chosen the wrong audience, he seemed to give the impression that the content of his speech was in some way too sophisticated for the audience gathered. It did not occur to Blair that at least some of his audience were registering their political opposition to what he said.

Communication and healthcare workers

Communication in a healthcare setting is important not only to transmit information to the patient but also to assist medical professionals in determining their diagnosis and treatment. We saw when discussing emotional labour (see chapter 2) how doctors can become stressed because of the emotional wear and tear involved in expressing suitable emotions to their patients. Worthington (2008) claims that volunteers in hospices can sometimes find themselves working as intermediaries between the families of patients and the medical staff. In her view, these volunteers need to have well-developed listening skills, be able to detect the strength of the feelings of families, appreciate different cultural expressions of suffering and be able to empathise with patients and their families. This is defined as active empathetic listening and involves being able to decipher emotional subtexts and is '. . . based upon one's ability to sense, process, and respond to incoming messages' (Worthington, 2008, p. 29). Although there are no doubt ways to teach people to detect these emotional subtexts, individuals will still vary in the depth of their understanding and in what they choose to do with information they receive.

Communication and the police

Communication skills have become increasingly important for police officers in the era of community policing. Woods (2000) conducted a series of interviews with police officers participating in a training scheme and found that they ranked listening skills above their abilities to question, inform and observe non-verbal communication. When asked about the skills required to transmit information, they noted that their priority was to make themselves clear though this was followed closely by the need to monitor their own emotions and to keep these under control. Schneider (1999) claims that community policing initiatives in socially disadvantaged areas are often hampered because of a mismatch between the communication strategies used by the residents and police. His research took place in a low-income neighbourhood in East Vancouver which contained a high immigrant population and had high levels of unemployment, drug use, street prostitution and gang-related crime. Some communication problems stemmed from language and cultural differences between the predominantly English-speaking police force and residents from diverse ethnic backgrounds, and these differences were exacerbated because police officers were regarded with suspicion by many of the new arrivals. Indeed, because of the '... fear and trepidation that many immigrants may feel towards agents of the state, police automatically enter into an asymmetrical power relationship with these groups that may distort communication' (Schneider, 1999, p. 357). He points out that the language used by the police is tinged by the relative power they possess and this can create resistance within deprived areas. Although the police expected cooperation from the neighbourhood and received plenty of information about crimes and antisocial behaviour taking place, the police were found to be remiss in feeding back to the community. What both pieces of research show in different ways is that the police might be involved in developing their listening skills, but barriers to effective communication remain because the police want information but will not necessarily open themselves up to scrutiny by members of the community.

The literature on improving communication skills draws attention to the importance of being concise and clear in the messages we transmit, whilst being sensitive to the audience and to the opinions expressed by other people. This approach to communication tends to focus upon the individual as an active agent, but it is equally as important to consider communication within a group setting. We have seen, for example, that teams can serve to filter messages and censor out anything regarded as a threat to their interests. Examples provided on the use of communication skills in health care illustrate the importance of reading emotions as well as simply processing the words transmitted. We have also seen that communication can be hampered because of inequalities in power stemming from hierarchies at work, standing in the community, the ability to punish and even the unequal possession of cultural capital. We have approached some of these issues when looking at power earlier in this volume (see chapters 4 and 5) and when considering possible barriers to effective intervention in the community (see chapter 6). Paying attention to the development of communication skills is important in the context of working in teams and with the public, but the broader sociopolitical context should also be taken into account if progress is to be made.

Conclusion

If given positions of responsibility, workers need to be aware of the leadership abilities they possess and how these abilities can be enhanced. They need to know that their authority will probably be challenged and that they will have to learn how to remain focused, coordinate teams, manage problems and use their insight to balance conflicting interests and demands. They need to recognise, moreover, that they can only lead because of the support given to them by others. Rather than think solely in terms of the abilities of an individual, it is important to be aware of how individuals are also helped by teams. One of the problems with attempting to consider ways to enhance employability skills is that it can give the impression that the individual is free to determine how these skills are developed. This is far from the case. Individuals learn from participating in teams and how they make use of the collective memory and pool of experience within a team. They will also learn from interacting with others and from attempting to find their place in a team structure. This learning experience takes place even when a team is dysfunctional. Individuals also learn from communicating with others, as they will need to discover how to make sense of what others say and how to respond appropriately. They will see what they need to do to argue a case and how this differs from finding ways to resolve disputes. Good communication relies upon people being clear about what they want to say and committing themselves to understanding, as best they can, the messages they receive and the audiences they address. Although leadership, teamwork and communication are skills which can be valued in their own right, they are also extremely important in how they impact upon approaches to problem solving, decision making and creative thinking. These skills will be discussed in the next chapter.

Questions to consider

1. What is the difference between leadership and management?
2. What, if anything, can be done to alleviate conflict in teams?
3. What are the main barriers to effective communication?

A guide to reading

General works that cover leadership, teamwork and communication include Berkun (2008), Lock (2007), Mersino (2007) and Hind and Moss (2011). More specialised research on leadership includes Williams (2005), which looks at the views of company directors. Fisher (2009) and Gau and Company (2007) explore the leadership skills needed by social workers and Ansari (2009) looks at leadership in health care. Belbin (2010) is useful as an introduction to understanding roles in teams, whilst conflict in teams is examined by Billingham (2008) and Spolander and Martin (2012). Chan (2002) provides a good introduction to communication. The importance of communication in health care is covered by Worthington (2008) and in the police service by Woods (2000) and Schneider (1999).

learning through work

References

Ansari, W. (2009) 'Joint working for health and social outcomes: The partnership-leadership mantra', *International Journal of Leadership in Public Services*, Volume 5, Issue 1, pp. 29–36.

Beamish, A. (2008) *Learning from Work: Designing Organizations for Learning and Communication*, Stanford Business Books: Stanford, CA.

Belbin, R.M. (2010) *Team Roles at Work*, Elsevier: Oxford.

Berkun, S. (2008) *Making Things Happen: Mastering Project Management*, O'Reilly: Cambridge.

Billingham, V. (2008) *Project Management*, Studymates Publishing: Abergele.

Bjerlov, M. and Docherty, P. (2006) 'Collective Reflection under ambiguity'. In D. Boud, P. Cressey and P. Docherty (eds) *Productive Reflection at Work*, Routledge: London, pp. 29–42.

Blair, T. (2010) *A Journey*, Arrow Books: London.

Branson, R. (2008) *Business Stripped Bare*, Virgin Books: London.

Chan, J.F. (2002) *Communication Skills for Managers*, American Management Association: New York.

Engelbrecht, L. (2012) 'Project management across diverse Cultures'. In G. Spolander, G. and L. Martin, L. (eds) (2012) *Successful Project Management in Social Work and Social Care*, Jessica Kingsley: London, pp. 148–161.

Ferguson, A. (2013) *My Autobiography*, Hodder and Stoughton: London.

Fisher, E. (2009) 'Motivation and leadership in social work management: A review of theories and related studies', *Administration in Social Work*, Volume 33, Issue 4, pp. 347–367.

Gau, K. and Company, J. (2007) 'Leaders in hospital based social work', *Leadership in Health Services*, Volume 20, Issue 2, pp. 124–133.

Hillmore, P. (1985) *Live Aid: The Greatest Show on Earth*, London: Sidgwick & Jackson.

Hind, D. and Moss, S. (2011) *Employability Skills*, Business Education Publishers: Houghton le Spring.

Howe, J., Hyer, K., Mellor, J., Lindeman, D. and Luptak, M. (2001) 'Educational approaches for preparing social work students for interdisciplinary teamwork on geriatric healthcare teams', *Social Work in Health Care*, Volume 32, Issue 4, pp. 19–42.

Lock, D. (2007) *Project Management*, Gower: Aldershot.

Melton, J. (2003) 'When teams work best', *Business Communication Quarterly*, Volume 66, pp. 133–138.

Mersino, A. (2007) *Emotional Intelligence for Project Managers*, Amacom: New York.

Ohlsson, J. (2013) 'Team learning: Collective reflection processes in teacher teams', *Journal of Workplace Learning*, Volume 25, Issue 5, pp. 296–309.

Raelin, J.A. (2008) *Work-Based Learning: Bridging Knowledge and Action in the Workplace*, Jossey-Bass: San Francisco.

Schneider, S. (1999) 'Overcoming barriers to communication between police and socially disadvantaged neighbourhoods: A critical theory of community policing', *Crime, Law & Social Change*, Volume 30, pp. 347–377.

Spolander, G. and Martin, L. (2012) *Successful Project Management in Social Work and Social Care*, Jessica Kingsley: London.

Templar, R. (2003) *The Rules of Work*, Pearson: Harlow.

chapter 9

Problem Solving, Decision Making and Creativity

In this chapter we look at problem solving, decision making and creativity, and we will consider some of the links between these skills. Problem solving and decision making are key skills for those who take on leadership responsibilities. Problems will arise at work and could include issues related to the management of personnel, to the efficient provision of a service or to the creation of a product. The term *problem solving* is used here to denote the development of solutions in response to acute incidents. *Decision making*, on the other hand, is viewed as an ongoing process and will include minor decisions made each day about how to set priorities as well as far-reaching decisions about the strategic direction of an organisation. In the case of both decision making and problem solving, it is important to deconstruct problems, consider a range of possible responses and select an appropriate solution. At the outset, it might be worth noting that problem solving and decision making can be distinguished from one another by the degree of urgency involved. Whilst decision making can be incremental and does not necessarily involve the pressure of time or a crisis situation, problem solving often starts with a negative situation and looks for a solution to reduce or to remove the problem completely. As we will see, problem solving and decision making can be a creative process in which people think freshly about issues in work and devise innovative solutions.

Problem solving

A survey of British companies conducted by the Confederation of British Industry revealed that 38% of employers felt that the problem-solving abilities of young people were inadequate and ill-suited to the demands of modern work (see Cassidy, 2014). Whilst the formal curriculum in most schools will include problem solving in various forms, especially when related to mathematics and science, there is still room for innovation in the way problem-solving skills are cultivated. It has been argued that chess should be made a compulsory part of the curriculum for primary school children in the belief that it can help to develop useful problem-solving abilities (Paton, 2014). Problem solving could be viewed like a formula and divided into identifying the problem, considering the options, making a choice and '. . . evaluation of what has been accomplished, what has been learned, and what it means' (Hoenig, 2000, p. 122). Problem solving does not end with the identification of a solution. Indeed, the importance of monitoring the implementation of the solution and reflecting upon its suitability, success and possible transferability are equally important.

Identifying problems

As problem solving must begin by identifying the problem, it is worth considering that what constitutes a problem will vary considerably across sectors and between people. A problem can be seen as the '. . . gap between an actual situation or the perception of it and the required or expected situation' (Maylor, 2010, p. 338). Expectations play an important role in determining whether a set of circumstances is regarded as problematic. For example, a school dedicated to releasing the creative abilities of its pupils might be less concerned with boisterous behaviour than one attempting to prepare its pupils for standard examinations and elite occupations. Some problems will be couched in personal terms. Sole traders, for example, need to consider their personal circumstances when making decisions about their own business. When Jeff Bezos created Amazon as on online bookstore in his garage, he did not make a profit for the first four years. In order to address this problem, he decided to offer a greater range of products. In constructing his list of products, he chose items that could be marketed efficiently using the World Wide Web. This created stable criteria for him to use in selecting the goods he would sell (see Hoenig, 2000). In the context of project management, Berkun (2008) notes that even the most experienced project managers and project teams will encounter difficulties and that project managers will have to take responsibility for finding solutions to these problems. He claims that when managers take responsibility for solving a problem, it enables team members to concentrate on their roles and it can reduce the negative impact of the problem. Managers will still be faced with the need to identify the criteria they use in solving problems. Should the interests of the organisation be placed above those of the client or of the staff? Although it could be argued that the organisation must prioritise protecting its own interests so that it can continue to employ people and respond to the market, it is also apparent that organisations are damaged by poor relations with employees and from failing to satisfy their clients.

When thinking in terms of problem solving, we need to be aware that problems can go undetected and unsolved. Berkun (2008) points out that problems do not necessarily have a definite beginning and end. Moreover, it could be that certain problems elude solutions and require constant management. This applies, for example, where colleagues find it hard to work together. Being able to distinguish between the symptoms and root causes of problems is an essential skill, for simply concentrating on the symptoms will lead to nothing more than a series of quick-fix solutions which invariably miss the mark. Taking time to identify the problem, communicating this to those who need to know and asking whether solutions are at hand or need to be devised would seem essential at the start of the problem-solving process.

Responding to problems

Maylor (2010) points out that problems vary in intensity and in the range of solutions that can be employed. Problem solving might require an instant response, allow for a short period of consultation or involve forward planning to deal with a problem which looks likely to emerge in the future. Depending on the situation, solutions can be immediate and instinctive or long term and methodical. Violent confrontation between colleagues, for example, would constitute a problem requiring an immediate solution in the majority of settings. A short period of consultation might be appropriate for reallocating responsibilities within a team. There will usually be a little more time to consider options if the problem is something that is likely to emerge in the future. Examples of such problems could include possible changes in funding for a third sector group following a change of government or a shift in the priorities of major grant awarding bodies. Planning to deal with long-term problems might involve this third sector group finding ways to create alliances with other groups or perhaps change the focus of the service it provides. These examples show that problem solving needs to take into account the likely impact of a problem in the short, medium and long term. There should be more opportunities for consultation and deliberation if the problem is one that might exist in the future but does not impact directly upon current work.

Procedures for solving problems

Procedures can be established for solving certain problems. In some cases, a particular response can be identified and used each time this problem arises. Once an issue has been identified, a 'programmed response' could be available. This might help to reduce the focus on the individual making the decision and concentrate more upon the way the organisation works (see Maylor, 2010). Devising solutions to problems should take into account prior experience and the particular needs of the situation. One way to identify possible solutions to problems is through discussions within a team. Maylor (2010) claims that it is sometimes useful to pull the team away from their immediate tasks and concerns and to share ideas, consider the future and focus upon particular problems. It is important to ensure that a variety of people contribute to the discussions and that people are allowed time to consider the issues. Managers should take note of all ideas and suggestions and treat each contribution with respect, so as to prevent dominant individuals or groups from taking over the process. Adopting a group approach to problem solving can help the group to form and take ownership of the solutions.

Implementing solutions

Having considered a range of options, it is then important to select the solution. Hind and Moss (2011) suggest that the best way to do this is to devise criteria against which all of the options can be considered. The solution can then be chosen in a clear and structured way. Applying a solution might require the release of resources and will usually need action on behalf of one or more individuals (see Hind and Moss, 2011). Once a solution has been implemented, its success needs to be evaluated. This will also help to determine if the solution could be used and adapted in response to a similar problem in the future. The purpose of the evaluation should be to determine the extent to which the solution was appropriate and succeeded in reducing the severity of the problem. Hind and Moss (2011) suggest that this can be done by comparing the outcomes and expected outcomes of a solution. If the outcomes yield considerably less than the expected outcomes, then the solution will have failed and the problem would need to be approached again.

Reflection and problem solving

Reflection can be used in problem solving to see whether it is appropriate or realistic to expect to find a solution. Moon (2004) notes that not all problems lend themselves to right or wrong answers. Ethical dilemmas are a case in point. In her view, it might be necessary to accept there are no correct solutions to problems and so evaluate problem solving in a different way. If the aim of the exercise is to evaluate how people construct knowledge and consider options, she claimed that some people will struggle with problems that elude a single solution. Others will accept some uncertainty but will argue their case in the belief that those who hold different views do so because of deficiencies in their reasoning. Finally, there are those who will reflect upon arguments whilst accepting there can be no final solution. It is clear that a team might include people who subscribe to these different approaches. Whilst some team members might look for instant solutions and be frustrated by people wanting to engage in lengthy arguments, there might be those who see a prolonged debate over the problem or possible solutions as a sign of a healthy organisation. Given such divisions, it is important for managers to find ways to accommodate both approaches.

Learning how to solve problems

The ability to solve problems should not be restricted to a small minority. Indeed, problem solving abilities should be encouraged throughout a team. According to Billett (1999), workers learn how to solve problems by noting the approaches taken by colleagues. Rather than relying upon formal guidance, the process of observing other workers as they tackle problems can empower workers and make the problems faced at work seem considerably less daunting. Matthews and Candy (1999) claim that workers will experiment at work rather than remain in their comfort zones. Through working in teams and observing one another, workers are said to generate new knowledge and add to the collective understanding of recurring problems. Consider, for example, the ways in which colleagues will share information about how to make use of technology. Workers might need to find out how to book their leave electronically. Although there might be some formal training available, workers will often find it quicker to ask for help from a colleague and might in turn be able to pass on their knowledge to others. By sharing experiences, workers can learn how to deal with problems together. They might develop ways to deal with problems within teams rather than involve management, if only to keep management at a distance. It is important to factor in the support provided by colleagues because it helps to avoid thinking about problem solving as the sole domain of management. Workers will often find ways to cooperate at work as a way to protect their own autonomy (see chapters 4–5) and to contribute towards the social capital (see chapter 6) of a workplace.

Teams and problem solving

Teams do not necessarily solve problems with due care. West (2012) notes that teams can sometimes defer to key individuals and ignore the contributions made by other people. Team members might also withhold their opinions if they feel that they are out of step with the views of the majority or the preferences of dominant individuals. Those of a lower status in an organisation might also be ignored by senior figures. Teams, moreover, can sometimes lose a sense of perspective and agree to foolish things. Majority opinion might disempower individuals and make them feel marginalised in the team. In some ways, the dominant opinion does not even have to be expressed. It is quite possible that team members will have assumptions about the views of a team and believe that there is a dominant view based perhaps upon previous meetings and the opinions expressed on similar issues in the past. It is also important to note that teams do not always possess the character and skills necessary for effective problem solving. Teams often want to explore solutions to problems before they have identified and unpacked the problem (see West, 2012). It could be that managers need to find ways to involve teams in problem solving, especially where teams are able to provide important information or have insight into key issues. From a management perspective, however, it is also important to manage expectations and avoid giving the impression that teams have complete autonomy. The participation of the team in problem solving rarely means that the team makes the final decision.

9a. Students on problem solving

The importance of urgency in problem solving can be illustrated by referring to the problems faced by a group of social science students when teaching in a local secondary school. Ria recalled that it was important to be flexible and respond to problems as they arise. In her first two teaching sessions, she encountered two main problems. During the first session, she discovered that YouTube was blocked within the school, which meant she was unable to use some of the visual aids she had identified. With ten minutes notice, she had to produce something to fill the time. In the second session, she discovered there were fewer students than expected. Once again she needed to adapt and reduce the number of subgroups and tasks to be performed. Anthony worked on the same project. He recalled that the project team became concerned over the behaviour of one pupil. Believing that their project was jeopardised by the disruption this pupil caused, members of the team recognised that something had to be done. They realised, however, that they had limited authority in the school. Knowing that they were upset by the experience, they agreed to discuss possible solutions the following day in the hope that they would be able to approach the problem in a more rational way (Anthony). These examples show that some problems need instant solutions and rely heavily upon the creative responses of an individual, whilst others can be dealt with in a more measured way and take into account the opinions of others.

It is important to see problem solving as a process which involves a series of stages that can be used continually in a work setting. These stages are quite straightforward in that they involve identifying a problem, considering alternatives and opting for a solution. Although this process might seem a little formulaic, subtleties are introduced as soon as we recognise variations in the way people interpret what constitutes a problem and the criteria used to pick a solution from a collection of alternatives. The reflective process (covered in detail in chapter 7) can also be used in problem solving and can help to deter people from always opting for a programmed response. We have also seen that problem solving should not be regarded as a purely managerial function and that this process seeps through places of work and can empower workers. It makes sense to see problem solving within the context of experiential learning, reflection, power, teamwork and decision making.

Decision making

As we have noted already, there are many links between decision making and problem solving. Decision making refers to the process by which decisions are made without necessarily being spurred on by the existence of a problem which must be overcome. Brunsson (2007) claims that decision making can be used to identify choices, but it can also be used to allocate resources within an organisation. By making this process transparent, it can help to give an organisation legitimacy. It is clear, however, that managers will avoid making decisions if they feel that there is insufficient support for their preferred option. It is also important to see many decisions are made by making use of, and responding to, scraps of information. As people often work with incomplete information, they need to determine how to judge the importance of the information they have (see Lock, 2007). Berkun (2008) notes that decision makers will often need to allow for diverse views and be able to show how these views have been considered in a fair and transparent way. It is important to know who has authority to make decisions and perhaps something about the foundations of this authority. Although the right to make decisions might be granted to an individual because of his or her place within a hierarchy, the ability to implement decisions will often rely upon the willingness of team members to cooperate.

As with problem solving, there are a number of stages involved in the decision-making process. Whereas problem solving begins with dissecting the problem, decision making can begin by asking whether a decision needs to be made. Berkun (2008) notes that decision makers need to consider the cost of making the wrong decision, the time available for making the decision and the experience they have in making similar decisions. They need to be aware of the degree of autonomy they have to make the decision and consider the possible impact of the decisions they make. These structural factors need to be taken into account before any options are considered. When choosing from a range of options, the decision maker should be willing to include the unattractive options and to consider each option in turn and have the confidence to choose the option with the greatest potential for success.

The importance of emotions

Most people do not process information and form conclusions in a purely rational way with little or no regard for how they feel. Although tapping into positive emotions can encourage people to stretch their capabilities and appeal to the best in others, the same cannot be said of negative emotions. Beard and Wilson (2006) claimed that negative emotions, such as fear and anger, can stand in the way of learning and can have a significant impact upon the way people interpret experiences. They argue that the cultivation of emotional intelligence is important to help individuals to overcome negative feelings at work and to develop positive approaches which can benefit the individual and the team. In their view, emotional intelligence can '. . . contribute to improved team morale, more collaborative working, less energy waste on politicking and game play, thus reducing poor attitude or indifference' (Beard and Wilson, 2006, p. 174). They also note that learners who enter higher education later in life often find that they have to battle with some of these negative emotions and that their student journey becomes extremely important for their evolving sense of identity. For these commentators, experiential learning and the way people interact with others should be grounded in understanding their own emotions and the emotions of others.

Decision making and emotional intelligence

The ability to make decisions can be improved by considering the impact of emotions. Indeed, it has been argued that when '. . . we are in touch with and able to access our emotions, we can leverage that information to make better decisions' (Mersino, 2007, p. 14). Recognising and addressing negative feelings, such as anger or fear, can help to inform decision making, whilst failure to do so can lead to poor or reactive decision making. The process of decision making also needs to consider the feelings of others. Being socially aware and empathetic helps leaders to understand what others may be experiencing and why. Although emotional states need to be taken into account, it does not mean that decisions should be made in a primarily emotional way. It is still important to make the best decision possible whilst considering the influence of the emotional dimension of a problem and its proposed solution (see Mersino, 2007, p. 182). Recognising the importance of emotions does not commit the decision maker to respond to the feelings of all concerned regardless of broader strategic aims. From a management perspective, it will always be important for organisations to have a clear sense of direction and to strive for a definable ethos. These can be communicated to workers with the knowledge that they will invariably have opinions and feelings towards what their employers are attempting to do. Although organisations do not have to be driven by the fluctuating emotions of their workers, ignoring these emotions can create problems for decision making and for the implementation of solutions.

Participation in decision making

The scope for individuals to be involved in making decisions will often depend upon their place in the hierarchy. Illeris (2011) notes that organisations range from those that operate in a hierarchal manner to those that allow for greater levels of autonomy. Whilst large organisations and those which embrace a bureaucratic structure tend to be far more hierarchal, small companies will tend to give more room for individuals to participate in decision making. Participation in decision making is not simply about having a say in a particular decision. It is far more about being able to contribute towards the ethos and personality of an organisation. By participating in decision making, workers can develop a sense of belonging and even start to draw connections between their own welfare and that of their employers. It is quite possible that workers will develop these emotional bonds more easily in small companies or organisations, where they feel that they matter and where they know the management personally or where the organisation is structured along cooperative lines. It might be asking rather more of workers who work in large, impersonal organisations and who feel that their opinions and welfare are ignored by their employers. It should be evident that such emotional bonds are unlikely to form in an organisation that disregards and disrespects its workers.

Decision making and work in the community

Engaging in the life of the community as an active citizen can help people to develop key skills in decision making. According to Putnam (2000), governments find it easier to govern when citizens are informed and able to participate in the democratic process. In his view, participating in small community ventures can be educational on a number of levels. Practical skills like learning how to run a meeting, speaking in public, writing letters, debating public issues and managing projects can be developed through participating in community ventures. People can also experience at first hand the importance of cooperation with others and can find ways to make their voices heard. Key political skills can also be developed through making use of bespoke toolkits. Organisations like Common Purpose, for example, have established Internet resources on the workings of parliament and local councils, how to start an ethical business and how to volunteer. Case studies have been developed on becoming a school governor, starting and maintaining a campaign, taking on a company or running a referendum (see Timmins, 2000). Organisations like Involve (see Involve, 2014) provide online resources on active citizenship and its implications for society. These resources can be accessed freely by people who want to learn how to take part in their communities.

It has been argued (see Furnham, 2008) that people who are serious about their responsibilities as citizens are often willing to contribute more to the corporate culture of the workplace by helping their colleagues and by taking on extra responsibilities. The extent to which this occurs, however, depends upon the way employers treat these active citizens. If people are satisfied and feel committed to their jobs, they are far more likely to participate and to give more back. Providing workers with rewards, involving them in decision making and acknowledging their contributions can help to encourage cooperation and even efficiency in the workplace. It might indeed make sense for employers to take note of the active citizens in their ranks and to invest in their development. By taking part in the community and developing the skills necessary to be active citizens, individuals will become more adept at dealing with different groups of people, situations and problems. These skills could be important in the workplace and should not be ignored by employers. It is important to realise, however, that this relies upon employers and managers understanding the benefits of active citizenship and their willingness to hand over some responsibility and control to those who have developed important skills in the community.

Decision making in teaching and the police

Participation in decision making has been shown to improve the experience of workers in teaching and in the police force. Weiss (1999) found that newly qualified teachers were far happier in schools if they were actively involved in decision making. These new teachers were particularly interested in putting forward their views on the curriculum, course content, teaching techniques and discipline. Involving teachers in decision making was found to be good for morale and made it far more likely that they would continue to develop their careers in teaching and look for ways to progress. Being able to exercise autonomy and participate in decision making offered teachers the opportunity to gain greater involvement in school leadership, which in turn created opportunities to take on new roles and responsibilities.

Similar benefits have been recorded in research on decision making and the police. Marks and Sklansky (2008) point out that community policing relies upon police officers taking greater initiative and relying less upon rigid command structures. They claim that this approach can often be undermined by colleagues who define their role as being one of enforcing the law rather than working with the community. Keith Smy (2007), the chief superintendent of Staffordshire Police, claimed in an article for the press that he wanted to move away from the command-and-control approach traditionally used in the police force and allow police officers to take a greater role in decision making. He believed that by encouraging participation in the decision-making process, his team adopted more positive attitudes towards their work. Steinheider and Wuestewald (2008) talked about the impact of a shared leadership scheme which was designed to give police officers greater autonomy and a more significant voice in the decision-making process. The Oklahoma Police Department made use of a leadership team, consisting of officers from across the department, to bridge the gap between senior management and frontline police officers. The recorded benefits of this scheme included improved communication, improved attitudes towards work and the spread of interest in the workings of management. Officers claimed that they preferred being consulted and felt they were valued and respected as colleagues. Retention rates for staff, job satisfaction and commitment to the group all improved.

We should note, however, that the decentralisation of power does not mean that all decisions are made democratically. The initiatives mentioned earlier allow for greater levels of participation in the decision-making process and for the cultivation of leaders at different levels of the organisation. Schemes such as these promote the value of leadership and attempt to encourage workers to take on greater levels of responsibility. They do not, however, transform leaders into mere delegates who have to obey the majority on each issue.

We have seen from the use of examples drawn from teaching and the police, that consulting workers in the decision-making process can lead to greater levels of fulfilment at work (this was covered in greater depth in chapter 3) and can even improve compliance with the decisions made. We should note, moreover, that emotions need to be considered when making decisions, because they will impact upon the decisions made and will be important when decisions are implemented. Failure to pay attention to the emotional dimension of decision making can only help to create the illusion that rational decisions will always be supported and followed. It might also be worth noting that workers will develop ways to resist the imposition of changes in the terms and conditions of their employment or in the methods used in the work they do (see chapter 5) and that one way to alleviate the sum of this resistance could be through allowing for the greater participation of workers in the decision-making process.

Creativity

In the final section of this chapter, we will take a look at the importance of creativity in problem solving, some methods used in creative thinking and some criticisms of creativity. A creative approach to problem solving involves a willingness to consider unconventional and novel ideas and to jettison previously held ideas if they are no longer relevant (McFadzean, 1999). Creative thinking can be used for '. . . the generating decomposing and analysing ideas/opportunities/solutions' (Cancer and Mulej, 2013, p. 68). The process involves using creativity to challenge existing ideas, to see problems in different ways or to make new connections between possible alternatives. By allowing creativity to develop in a group setting, it is hoped that impractical ideas will be aired but also rejected (see Cancer and Mulej, 2013). Problem solving should be a creative process in that it involves dissecting a problem and considering possible solutions. We have seen, however, that there is sometimes the preference for a programmed solution which involves responding to a problem in a familiar and predictable way.

Challenging paradigms

We should be aware that problem solving and decision making will often take place within the context of a paradigm or world view. Paradigms enshrine preferred ways of working and can be presented as a philosophy or set of principles. For example, a school could pride itself on its reputation in teaching the arts and sports. It might ensure that these subject areas are well resourced and develop useful links with universities offering these subjects so as to ease the way for its pupils. Changes in circumstances could, however, force the school to reconsider its dominant ethos or paradigm. It might have to change in response to government policy, to funding available for certain subjects, to the changing intake of the school, to the demands of parents and to the capabilities and interests of the children. Under these circumstances, the school would need to think creatively, because its existing paradigm could no longer accommodate the new pressures exerted on the school.

In order to think creatively, it is important for individuals to recognise the impact of these paradigms. It has been argued that '. . . creativity can be encouraged by changing a person's mindset or paradigm' (McFadzean, 1999, p. 374). She claimed that paradigms can be challenged by asking people to define the present situation, consider possible futures and then discuss the different terms used to describe the present and the future. This method, which could make use of drawings as prompts for discussion, is described as visioning and is considered important '. . . because it can help creative thinkers to break their paradigms and think of a more powerful future' (McFazdean, 1999, p. 381). According to McFazdean, sessions could be run in which workers were called upon to generate as many ideas as possible so that these ideas can be the raw material for groups to discuss creatively. This process allows people to take more chances and to think more creatively about possible solutions to problems by allowing one idea to spark other ideas (see Knippen and Green, 1997). Icebreakers could also be used to liberate the creative energies of the group. For example, each member of the group could be asked to make two statements to the group about themselves. One of these statements must be true and the other must be false. The rest of the group would have to determine which statement was true (see McFazdean, 1999). We should recognise that creative thinking does not suit all types of decision making. The majority of decisions will take place within established paradigms. The use of creative thinking is more suited to situations which call upon teams to abandon old ways of working and to think freshly in response to new problems.

Problems with creative problem solving and decision making

We need to avoid falling into the trap of equating the new with progress and overestimating the importance of creative approaches to decision making. Brown (1991) claims that creativity is not necessarily good, especially if it attempts to undermine methods of working that come naturally and are effective. He notes that those who wish to foist upon the world their innovations are often unmindful of the complexity involved in the paradigms created. McFadzean (1999) claims it is important to recognise the importance of comfort and to endeavour to find a suitable balance between comfort and creativity (McFadzean, 1999). We have seen that workers will often resist change and that change is usually supported by management if it promises to increase profitability, efficiency and perhaps their own place within an organisation. Because of this, there is no reason to believe that workers will want to support change, even if the decisions made were arrived at creatively.

We have seen that creativity can be important as a response to problems when established ways of working have been found to be ineffective. The starting point, however, should not be with the generation of new ideas but with recognising the paradigms within which people work and whether these paradigms are suited to changing conditions. We need to recognise that rapid change in processes of work can be alienating and pull individuals away from aspects of their work that they find fulfilling. This distinction between alienation and fulfilment has been explored elsewhere (see chapter 3), but it is something that needs to be considered in problem solving, decision making and in the use of creative methods.

Conclusion

By focusing upon the component parts of problem solving and decision making, we can see that they involve the unpacking of issues, considering a range of options and responses, making choices and evaluating the choices made. This process can be used in a variety of ways and is important to deal with immediate problems, as well as to coordinate the activities of a team and contribute towards the strategic development of an organisation. Those who make decisions must be aware of the extent of their own authority and be able to read their colleagues and involve them as needed in the decision-making process. Although it is no doubt the case that some decisions will be made by a small minority and filtered down through an organisation, isolated decision makers can encounter resistance from colleagues and problems in implementing their decisions. It makes sense, wherever possible, for the skills of problem solving and decision making to be disseminated within a team. These skills can empower individuals and encourage higher levels of engagement in the corporate life of an organisation. Although problem solving and decision making share many of the same characteristics, these two skills can be distinguished from one another by the character of the issues they face. Whilst problem solving starts with a negative situation and seeks to find solutions, decision making is something that can be applied across a broader range of issues. We have seen that creativity can be used in problem solving and decision making to unpack dominant paradigms and to generate new alternatives. In order to make effective use of these methods, it is important to evaluate the extent of the problems faced by an organisation before engaging in attempts to find creative solutions. Attitudes towards changes at work tend to be ambivalent at best, partly because of the existence of hierarchies and social inequalities but also because of the appeal of familiar methods of working. Even when organisations manage to introduce new and dynamic ways to deliver their product or service, resistance from within the workforce will take place. This is especially the case if change has led to increased demands being placed upon the workers.

Questions to consider

1. By what criteria should possible solutions to problems be judged?
2. What arguments can be made in favour of decentralising decision making?
3. Under what conditions should creative problem solving and decision making be used?

A guide to reading

For general works on problem solving and decision making see Hoenig (2000), Maylor (2010), Berkun (2008), Hind and Moss (2011), Brunsson (2007) and Lock (2007). For more specialised pieces on creativity see McFadzean (1999) and Cancer and Mulej (1999). Billett (1999) and Matthews and Candy (1999) have explored the importance of groups in problem solving. Moon (2004) looks at the role of reflection in problem solving, whereas Beard and Wilson (2006) and Mersino (2007) pay rather more attention to the importance of emotion in approaches to decision making. Sector examples on teaching can be found in Weiss (1999) and on the police in Marks and Sklansky (2008).

References

Beard, C. and Wilson, J. (2006) *Experiential Learning: A Best Practice Handbook for Educators and Trainers*, Kogan Page: London.

Berkun, S. (2008) *Making Things Happen: Mastering Project Management*, O'Reilly: Cambridge.

Billett, S. (1999) 'Guided learning at work'. In D. Boud and J. Garrick (eds) (1999) *Understanding Learning at Work*, Routledge: London, pp. 151–164.

Brown, M. (1991) 'Doubts: Some thoughts on the practice of creative problem-solving', *Leadership & Organization Development Journal*, Volume 12, Issue 6, pp. 15–17.

Brunsson, N. (2007) *The Consequences of Decision Making*, Oxford University Press: New York.

Cancer, V. and Mulej, M. (2013) 'Multi-criteria decision-making in creative problem solving', *Kybernetes*, Volume 42, Issue 1, pp. 67–81.

Cassidy, S. (2014) 'School leavers not ready for the world of work, says bosses', *The Independent*, 4 July 2014, p 14.

Furnham, A. (2008) 'Good citizens of the office can be cultivated through investment and training', *The Daily Telegraph*, 24 April 2008, p. 9.

Hind, D and Moss, S. (2011) *Employability Skills*, Business Education Publishers: Houghton le Spring.

Hoenig, C. (2000) *The Problem Solving Journey*, Perseus Publishing: Cambridge, MA.

Illeris, K. (2011) *The Fundamentals of Workplace Learning*, Routledge: London.

Involve (2014) http://www.involve.org.uk/blog/tag/unleashing-citizen-participation/ (last accessed 10 October 2014).

Knippen, J. and Green, T. (1997) 'Problem solving', *Journal of Workplace Learning*, Volume 9, Issue 3, pp. 98–99.

Lock, D. (2007) *Project Management, 9th Edition*, Gower: Aldershot.

Marks, M. and Sklansky, D. (2008) 'Voices from below: Unions and participatory arrangements in the police workplace', *Police Practice and Research: An International Journal*, Volume 9, Issue 2, pp. 85–94.

Matthews, J. and Candy, P. (1999) 'New dimensions in learning and knowledge'. In D. Boud and J. Garrick (eds) *Understanding Learning at Work*, Routledge: London, pp. 47–64.

Maylor, H. (2010) *Project Management*. Pearson: Essex.

McFadzean, E. (1999) 'Encouraging creative thinking', *Leadership & Organization Development Journal*, Volume 20, Issue 7, pp. 374–383.

Mersino, A. (2007) *Emotional Intelligence for Project Managers*, Amacom: New York.

Moon, J. (2004) *A Handbook of Reflective and Experiential Learning*, RoutledgeFalmer: Oxford.

Paton, G. (2014) 'Make chess compulsory for seven year olds at school, says teachers' leader', *The Daily Telegraph*, 17 April 2014, p.14.

Putnam, R. D. (2000) *Bowling Alone: The Collapse and Revival of American Community*, Simon and Schuster Paperbacks: New York.

Smy, K. (2007) 'What worked for us', *The Times*, 23 January 2007, p. 16.

Steinheider, B. and Wuestewald, T. (2008) 'From the bottom-up: Sharing leadership in a police agency', *Police Practice and Research*, Volume 9, Issue 2, pp. 145–163.

Timmins, N. (2000) 'INSIDE TRACK: Click here for a better life: CITIZENSHIP AND THE INTERNET: Active Citizenship has just become easier, thanks to a 'dangerous idea' that helps people and groups to share information', *The Financial Times*, 18 October 2000, p. 22.

Weiss, E.M. (1999) 'Perceived workplace conditions and first-year teachers' morale, career choice commitment, and planned retention: a secondary analysis', *Teaching and Teacher Education*, Volume 15, pp. 861–879.

West, M. (2012) *Effective Teamwork: Practical Lessons from Organizational Research*, Wiley: Hoboken.

chapter 10

Skills, Internships and Employability

It should be evident from what we have covered that the skills needed for graduate-level work should not be treated as separate and distinct bodies of knowledge but as skills which develop through practice and often rely upon working with other people. Couched within a framework of experiential learning and reflection, we have looked at a range of skills and suggested ways in which these skills could be developed in a work setting. It is important to note that work-related learning may well provide people with the experience to secure a particular job, although its value more often than not lies in providing them with a range of transferrable skills and in improving their employability. Work-related learning allows people to develop their understanding of the skills they have, how these have been developed and how they can be enhanced in the future. The reflective process can be particularly useful in identifying skills and attributes and in articulating these to a third party. The development of one's employability is not about learning a particular set of skills sealed forever, but it is contingent upon being willing to adapt to new challenges and recognising that careers are never more than a work in progress. This chapter will take a closer look at the relationship between skills and employability and will consider the value placed upon internships as a stepping stone to graduate-level work.

Skills

We have seen in previous chapters that, through work-related learning, individuals can develop a range of skills suitable for the modern work setting. By engaging with others at work, people can gain an appreciation of styles of leadership, decision making, problem solving, teamwork and communication. Although this list is by no means exhaustive, it does provide some illustrations of how individuals can hone their skills in preparation for graduate-level employment. We have taken a look at these skills from a variety of angles and have shown how they are important in different sectors of employment. To develop these skills, people need to make the best of their experiences and be able to identify ways to improve their performance. It should be evident also that they need to be reasonably confident about their skills if they are to convince others that they are capable of working at a higher level and thus advance in their careers (see de Botton, 2009).

The skills agenda in Britain

Whilst the ability of graduates to gain employment was something of a presumption amongst higher education institutions before the growth of the sector in the early 1990s, this convention was soon replaced by the belief that UK graduates needed to offer something more in order to compete globally (Mason et al., 2003). Although purists might wish to argue that the function of education is to illuminate understanding and to equip individuals with the ability to think in a variety of ways, this does not necessarily preclude the importance of developing transferable skills. The National Committee of Inquiry into Higher Education (1997) argued that universities need to respond to the challenges of the global economy and place greater attention on the cultivation of skills needed in the workplace. It has been argued that '. . . governments have an interest in obtaining better value for money from their higher education institutions and ensuring that students obtain a form of education that equips them with the skills on which the prosperity of a knowledge economy rests' (Symes, 2001, p. 207). British universities are increasingly expected to provide students with skills for the workplace in addition to those associated with studying a traditional academic subject (see Mason et al., 2003; Mason et al., 2006). Consecutive governments have therefore attempted to implement policies to encourage universities to consider the needs of employers and the economy (Scesa and Williams, 2007). We should be aware, however, that the skills needed by employers are changing constantly. Raelin (2008) argues that the skills gained at school are generally out of date by the time individuals enter employment and start building their careers. He claims that the majority of young people will have up to six or seven different careers throughout their lives, which will invariably require the cultivation of new skills. Because of this, employers are particularly interested in recruiting workers who are able to adapt to the needs of the organisation. Adaptability, indeed, could be regarded as an important feature of the skills workers develop. Rather than think in terms of learning all they can about particular skills, as if they are set in stone, people will benefit far more from considering how they have developed these skills in the past, how they look in the present and how they can develop these in the future.

Skills and stratification at work

Stratification at work often rests upon the kind of skills people have and how they use them. Winch (2000) notes that employers tend to have fairly low expectations of their workers involved in low-skilled work. These workers do not need to have progressed very far in their formal education and are expected to fit into work with relatively little training. Employers tend to accept that there will be a relatively high level of turnover in their staff base. Access to the professions, however, will depend, to a far greater extent, on the possession of qualifications. Winch (2000) points out that skilled workers are those who have developed the ability to perform specific functions through their education and training. The professions in particular rely upon a high level of training and the cultivation of a particular professional ethic. Expectations are placed upon doctors, for example, to be hard-working, patient and disciplined in their personal lives and many professions require workers to improve constantly and engage in continuing professional development. Although there are clearly differences between low-skilled work and the professions, especially in terms of salary and status, the distinction rests far more on formal qualifications.

Vocational education

Winch (2000) argues that there is a vocational dimension to all education, in the sense that it helps people to prepare for life. Vocational education differs from liberal education, however, because of the emphasis placed upon preparing people for their working lives. Vocational educators are prone to consider what is useful for a particular job, though this can mean finding ways to empower people and make them more valuable to employers. Winch goes on to argue that education and training are not mutually exclusive. Education can contain an element of training and training an element of education, but a distinction can still be made between education designed to prepare an individual for life and training designed to introduce an individual to a technique necessary to perform a particular job. The latter can be enhanced through workplace learning, where adults learn how to produce a particular item or deliver a particular service. Although vocational education differs from education designed to enhance the personal development of an individual, it does in many ways proceed from the assumption that '. . . trainees already have a level of autonomy and responsibility which affects the way in which they learn and can be taught' (Winch, 2000, p. 97).

Given this, it would appear that vocational education is a supplement to formal education, rather than an alternative to it. Running through this book is a belief that social science courses can benefit from the integration of a vocational element. This vocational element should not be introduced at the expense of diluting the academic content of the degrees. Indeed, by approaching work by making use of social scientific concepts (see chapters 2–6) it is hoped that students will see that work is a legitimate area of study and relevant to their own social scientific discipline.

The problems with vocational education

Education that aims primarily to prepare people to perform a particular job can be problematic. It has been argued (see Tomlinson, 2013) that non-professional vocational education is used to reinforce existing social divisions and inequalities by channelling some people to learn practical skills, whilst leaving a more privileged minority to concentrate upon their own academic learning. He notes that, in order to gain access to the professions, individuals need to engage with an abstract academic curriculum. In this way, some people are '. . . groomed for the types of skills and learning contexts that facilitate access to higher-level occupational pursuits' (Tomlinson, 2013, p. 98). There might be additional problems with vocational education, especially when this takes place in universities. By focusing the attention of students upon those skills necessary for work, vocational education can limit the curriculum and ignore some of the broader foundations of academic disciplines. Vocational courses might also prepare people for a narrow range of occupations and thereby marginalise these graduates in the labour market. This could be damaging if particular occupations are adversely affected by problems in the economy. If there is a slump in the housing market, for example, graduates in construction management might find it difficult to secure suitable work. Vocational education might also concentrate too much upon a narrow range of skills, whilst ignoring the importance of employability. Equipping somebody with the skills necessary to function in a particular occupation does not necessarily make them more employable.

When looking at the skills agenda in Britain, we need to remember that this agenda is set by the government in response to the supposed needs of employers. This agenda could be viewed as something imposed upon universities and students, but it is evident that graduates will need to compete in a market dominated by employers who are aware of what they require and will assume that university graduates should have at least some career management skills and an understanding of their own abilities. As the needs of employers are constantly changing, universities are increasingly expected to provide their students with the skills necessary to become reflective practitioners. Whilst in no way committing ourselves to vocational education, the argument contained herein recognises the importance of a vocational element within social science education and considers some of the ways to prepare social science graduates for the graduate labour market.

Internships

Internships, where students are provided with opportunities for unpaid or low-paid work, have become increasingly used by students to gain an advantage in the job market. In the United States, less than 3% of college students took part in internships in the early 1980s. By 2012, over 70% of college students claimed that they were actively seeking opportunities as an intern (Hurst, Good and Gardner, 2012). Internships have also become popular in Britain. *The Telegraph* points out that interns have a greater chance of securing graduate-level work and that a staggering 75% of graduate jobs in the city of London will go to those who have already served an internship (Stanford, 2014). Viewed very much from the perspective of employers, internships are supported as a way for employers to see candidates on a trial basis and to treat the internship like a lengthy interview (Bray, 2014). In what follows, we will take a look at the benefits of internships for students and employers and consider some of the problems with this system of employment.

Internships and students

Internships have been shown to increase the chances of students finding well-paid and graduate-level work (Holyoak, 2013). Part of the reason for this is that internships serve as a prolonged induction into possible careers and a way for students to develop important work-related skills. Maertz, Stoeberl and Marks (2014) claimed that internships help students to recognise what is required in particular industries and will help students to see the value of their own academic studies. They provide students with ways to develop communication and critical thinking skills and to bridge the gap between university and the world of work. But the value of internships to students stretches beyond the cultivation of particular skills. According to Hurst et al. (2012), students also become better at making informed choices about their careers and approaches to work as a result of working as an intern. Viewed in this way, internships can be seen as a way for students to sample possible careers and to acquaint themselves with the demands of professional careers.

Internships and employers

Employers are willing to provide internships for students because they represent a low-risk strategy to sample the next cohort of graduates. According to Maertz et al. (2014), internships provide employers with an opportunity to assess the value of potential recruits and to save in their training and recruitment of new employees. Having access to interns also enables employers to deal with projects they would not normally prioritise but that could be of value in the medium and long term. Hurst et al. (2012) notes that employers are particularly interested in having the chance to check if the intern has '. . . the qualities necessary to adapt to the firm's culture' (Hurst et al., 2012, p. 505). Employers do, however, claim that supervising interns who have poor work-related skills can be a draining experience and one which detracts from the potential value of having student interns (Maertz et al., 2014). It should be clear that employers have relatively little to lose by providing students with internships. They have no obligation to employ the interns at the end of the period or upon graduation and can cherry-pick their graduate recruits in this way.

Problems with internships

The Guardian has been critical of the use of interns, has covered some of the abuses of the system and has looked favourably on those who campaign for the abolition of these unpaid positions (see Malik, 2011). In addition to providing a source of cheap labour, internships have been criticised for failing to train students and because employers use their labour to undermine the bargaining rights of their paid employees (Winter, 2011). It is clear that the expectations of students and employers are very different. Whilst employers are primarily interested in having an extra pair of hands, students are understandably looking for development opportunities and will expect relevant training. When this training is not provided, students are apt to view their internship in a negative light (see Maertz et al., 2014). Holyoak (2013) interviewed 56 interns and supervisors and showed that the intrinsic value of an internship depended on the commitment and energy of their supervisors, as well as the attitudes of the interns themselves.

The debates over the value of internships rest upon different ideas about the responsibilities of employers. Seen from the perspective of employers, they are providing the opportunity for valuable experience and relevant training to students eager to improve their prospects of employment. There is no guarantee, however, that students will get this relevant training, and they will have to endure the experience of working without pay and without rights as an employee. Viewed within the context of issues covered in this book, we can see that internships might be particularly good at giving students socialisation into work and into particular occupational cultures (see chapter 2), whilst also providing some insight into inequalities in power (see chapter 4). We saw how working in the community can illuminate a range of social issues and help to solidify some of the academic material covered in social science education (see chapter 6). Viewed in this light, internships can have educational value beyond the skills accumulated and contacts made. In addition to helping to consolidate these features of an education in the social sciences, internships might also help to enhance the employability of the student.

Employability

The nurturing of student employability has become an important feature of higher education in Britain. Employability has been defined as '. . . a set of achievements – skills, understandings and personal attributes – that makes graduates more likely to gain employment and be successful in their chosen occupations, which benefits themselves, the workforce, the community and the economy' (Yorke, 2006, p. 8). This definition stresses that employability does not refer solely to the acquisition of a graduate-level job, but is concerned far more with the potential a graduate has to find suitable employment and to function well in this work. Helyer (2010) notes that in order to be employable in a contemporary context, workers need to be self-aware, adaptable and be able to reinvent themselves as the nature of their work changes. Graduates need to be aware of the needs of the labour market and have some insight into their own strengths and potential. Whilst in the short term individuals might want to identify the skills and dispositions they have and match these to the current labour market, in the long term it might make more sense for workers to identify what they want to achieve at work and then reflect upon the steps they need to take to reach their goals. This is not simply about rising through the ranks and becoming more successful in a traditional sense. Workers might, indeed, focus far more on maximising the fulfilment they feel at work. This could spur them into making sideways moves or even abandoning some of the responsibilities and seniority they currently have in the hope of finding more interesting things to do. People might choose to change occupations and pursue their dreams. All of these possibilities could be accommodated within a broad definition of employability.

Employability and the changing nature of work

The notion of employability can assist individuals in making choices in an increasingly fluid and flexible labour market. It has been argued (see Tomlinson, 2013) that the transition from a traditional modern industrial economy to the contemporary knowledge-based economy places fresh demands upon workers. They find that they have to develop their skills constantly and adapt to the changing demands of their employers. Having successfully studied for a degree reveals much about the abilities and skills of graduates.

Graduates are twice as more likely to find work than those with no qualifications and will tend to have the skills necessary to adjust to new approaches to work (Leitch Review of Skills, 2006). It has been estimated that at least half of the new jobs created in Britain by 2020 will be filled by graduates (Department for Innovation, Universities and Skills, 2008). We have seen that individuals can prepare themselves for new challenges by becoming more aware of their skills and developing these to make themselves more attractive in the labour market. But employability means rather more than this. Employability entails having an awareness of the skills and attributes required in the modern work setting and how these must change over time. Employability is, in many ways, a state of mind. It allows individuals to locate themselves within the context of their own career and within the broader economic, social and political climate.

Employability and career management

According to Tomlinson (2013), employability has become important because there is an increasing expectation that individuals will take responsibility for their own career progression. Workers are expected to understand the sector within which they work, key developments in their sector and the ways in which they can progress. Workers are encouraged to take responsibility for developing their own skills. Those who can anticipate the needs of their employers, and develop the skills necessary to serve these needs, tend to do well in their careers. The logical progression of a career path has given way to a more fluid system in which individuals manage their own abilities and interact with their employers in a more proactive way (see Tomlinson, 2013). Rather than think in terms of a set group of skills necessary to perform a particular job, it is important to develop through reflection, experience, learning and adapting to the changing demands of work (see Raelin, 2008). In this way, workers can learn to manage their careers and take a long view of what they would like to do and the skills they will need. It is worth bearing in mind that individuals will enter careers with different expectations. Young graduates entering the professions often find that they have to devise their own particular approach to their work and think about what they want to achieve in their careers.

Teaching and career development

Smethem (2007) investigated the views and attitudes of 18 newly qualified modern language teachers in relation to their work and the expectations they had of their careers. Smethem distinguished between three types of teacher. *Career teachers* were defined as those committed to teaching and who held ambitions for promotion. *Classroom teachers* were those identified as being happy to remain teaching in the classroom but not necessarily on a full-time basis. *Portfolio teachers* saw teaching as a step towards other careers. In each case, the teachers claimed they were motivated by the challenges and rewards of making an important contribution to society, working with young people, building relationships with pupils and improving teaching and learning. All of the teachers spoke of wanting to make a difference and felt that teaching offered a valuable and altruistic career choice. It is clear, however, that they viewed their own career progression in different ways and that this in turn would influence how receptive they are to developing their skills and their own continuing professional development. Whilst classroom teachers might focus upon developing further expertise in their own disciplines, those seeking to advance through to management would be more likely to seek to develop a different range of skills.

Social work and career development

The desire to make a positive contribution to society is also an important motivating factor for those who want a career in social work. In a review of what motivates people to want to study for a degree in social work, Gilligan (2007) noted that the majority of candidates responded to questions about the origins of social problems with suggestions about how the social problems could be alleviated. In the bulk of these cases, they attributed social problems to individual behaviour and believed that the intervention of professionals was necessary to correct this behaviour. This way of seeing social ills was far more common than one which focused primarily upon inequalities within the system. In a similar study, Furness (2007) claimed that students studying social work were driven primarily by the belief that they could help people to improve the quality of their lives rather than to take on systemic problems. Both studies revealed that people have different motivations for wanting a career in social work and it is likely that the expectations they have when entering a career will be challenged as a result of their experiences in the sector. Although it is possible for people to manage their own careers to an extent, it is also clear that they will never have total autonomy over their careers. This is particularly the case when these careers involve dealing with the emotions of others (see chapter 2).

Problems with employability

The concept of employability is not without its critics. Employability could be seen as a corporate ploy designed to squeeze more from their employees (see Tomlinson, 2013). It should be evident, however, that the value of the concept of employability depends upon what it includes and how it is used. If employability is viewed from the perspective of employers, then it is possible to see that employability could be reduced to a wish list and imposed upon workers. If this is the case, then employability can be seen as yet another stick with which to beat workers. But if employability is viewed within the context of an individual's self-development, the political significance of employability is transformed. By learning how to reflect upon experiences of work and to make realistic plans for the future, workers can take more control over the skills they choose to develop and the direction they take. In this way, the focus upon employability can be empowering.

In order to judge the value of employability as an organising concept, it needs to be considered in relation to broader debates about the functions of education. In drawing a distinction between liberal education, conservative education and radical education, Winch (2000) shows that each of these approaches to education has a different way of viewing personal development. Liberal educators are primarily concerned with helping individuals reach their potential and with finding ways to assist in personal development. Advocates of liberal education will place value upon equipping people to live autonomous and independent lives. This differs from conservative education, which concentrates in the main upon individuals acquiring knowledge and an appreciation of traditional cultural values. Rather than seek to encourage students to question, conservative educators prefer to create a more compliant citizenry. Radical educators, on the other hand, tend to regard education as a means by which individuals can learn to scrutinise society and contribute towards social change (see Winch, 2000). From what has been said already, it should be clear that employability does not fit neatly into only one of these perspectives on education. Employability can be seen as part of a liberal agenda, with its focus upon individuals pursuing their interests and developing their abilities. It can also be seen as a conservative tool to create workers who will serve dominant economic interests. Finally, it can be viewed in a radical light as a way to encourage people to become far more aware of the skills they have and how these can be used in the struggle for social justice. Employability can, indeed, be seen as being compatible with radically different ideas about the functions of education.

Conclusion

In this chapter, we have attempted to show some of the ways to view the relationship between skills and employability, and we have taken a look at some of the advantages and disadvantages of internships. We have argued throughout that work-related skills should not be seen as separate or self-contained and that each skill will feed into others. We have also attempted to show the links between employability and personal development and have argued that a person's employability can be viewed as part of his or her character rather than as something existing solely in a formal curriculum vitae. It is important that individuals learn from experience and treat these experiences with respect in an educational setting. Through reflecting upon what they do and how they do it, workers can gain a richer understanding of their own working lives and identify some ways to develop their interests at work. This might be through the cultivation of particular skills, but the decisions they make should be guided by the way they view their employability. Although employability includes a skills dimension, it is also a framework within which workers can scrutinise their experiences, attributes, attitudes and awareness of the demands and opportunities afforded by work. It is something that allows people to think about what they want, why they want it and how it relates to the way they view the world. This is not a recipe for individuals to pursue their interests regardless of everybody else, but for people to think about their value system and its relationship to the work they do.

Questions to consider

1. To what extent should universities respond to the needs of employers?
2. Are internships just another form of exploitation?
3. What is the relationship between employability and personal development?

A guide to reading

For general discussions on skills and employability, see Mason et al. (2003 and 2006), Raelin (2008) and Helyer (2010). Yorke (2006) provides a useful starting point for discussions on employability, whilst the foundation for the skills agenda in Britain can be seen in the National Committee of Inquiry into Education (1997) and the Leitch Review of Skills (2006). Useful critiques can be found in Winch (2000) and Tomlinson (2013). For the relationship between skills and career development in particular sectors, see Smethem (2007) on teachers and Gilligan (2007) on social workers.

References

Bray, P. (2014) 'Experience that will give them the edge', *The Daily Telegraph*, parents' guide section, 26 July 2014, p. 15.

de Botton, A. (2009) *The Pleasures and Sorrows of Work*, Hamish Hamilton: London.

Department for Innovation, Universities and Skills (2008) *Higher Education at Work Higher Skills: Higher Values*, http://www.dius.gov.uk/consultations/documents/Higher_Education_at_Work.pdf (last accessed 8 June 2009).

Furness, S. (2007) 'An enquiry into students' motivations to train as social workers in England', *Journal of Social Work*, Volume 7, pp. 239–253.

Gilligan, P. (2007) 'Well motivated reformists or nascent radicals: How do applicants to the degree in social work see social problems, their origins and solutions?' *British Journal of Social Work*, Volume 37, pp. 735–760.

Helyer, R. (2010) 'Adapting to higher education: Academic skills'. In R. Helyer (ed) (2010) *The Work Based Learning Student Handbook*, Palgrave Macmillan: Basingstoke, 2010, pp. 10–62.

Holyoak, L. (2013) 'Are all internships beneficial learning experiences? An exploratory study', *Education + Training*, Volume 55, Issue 6, pp. 573–583.

Hurst, J., Good, L. and Gardner, P. (2012) 'Conversion intentions of interns: What are the motivating factors?', *Education + Training*, Volume 54, Issue 6, pp. 504–522.

Leitch Review of Skills (2006) *Prosperity for all in the global economy – world class skills*, Crown copyright, Viewed at: http://www.hm-treasury.gov.uk/d/leitch_finalreport051206.pdf (last accessed 11 January 2012).

Maertz, C., Stoeberl, P. and Marks, J. (2014) 'Building successful internships: Lessons from the research for interns, schools, and employers', *Careers Development International*, Volume 19, Issue 1, pp. 123–142.

Malik, S. (2011) 'HMRC criticised overpayments of interns', *The Guardian*, 8 April 2013, p. 19.

Mason, G., Williams, G., Cranmer, S. and Guile, D. (2003) *How much does higher education enhance the employability of graduates?* Higher Education Funding Council for England, Viewed at: http://www.hefce.ac.uk/Pubs/rdreports/2003/rd13_03/rd13_03a.pdf (last accessed 10 June 2009).

Mason, G., Williams, G. and Cranmer, S. (2006) *Employability Skills Initiatives in Higher Education: What Effects Do They Have On Graduate Labour Market Outcomes?* National Institute of Economic and Social Research, London, Viewed at: http://www.niesr.ac.uk/pdf/061006_91251.pdf (last accessed 10 June 2009).

National Committee of Inquiry into Higher Education (1997) *Higher education in the learning society*, https://bei.leeds.ac.uk/Partners/NCIHE/

Raelin, J.A. (2008) *Work-Based Learning: Bridging Knowledge and Action in the Workplace*, Jossey-Bass: San Francisco.

Scesa, A. and Williams, R. (2007) 'Engagement in course development by employers not traditionally involved in higher education: Student and employer perceptions of its impact'. In *Research Evidence in Education Library*. EPPI-Centre, Social Science Research Unit, Institute of Education, University of London: London, http://eppi.ioe.ac.uk/cms/LinkClick.aspx?fileticket=yam9TACKRSM%3d&tabid=2316&mid=4281&language=en-US

Smethem, L. (2007) 'Retention and intention in teaching careers: Will the new generation stay?' *Teachers and Teaching: Theory and Practice*, Volume 13, pp. 465–480.

Stanford, P. (2014) 'Jobs at the end of the pipeline: Undergraduate should not underestimate the importance of internships', *The Daily Telegraph*, 25 January 2014, weekend section, p. 13.

Symes, C. (2001) 'Capital degrees: Another episode in the history of work and learning'. In D. Boud and N. Solomon (eds) (2001) *Work-Based Learning: A New Higher Education?* The Society for Research into Higher Education and Open University Press: Berkshire.

Tomlinson, M. (2013) *Education, Work and Identity*, Bloomsbury: London.

chapter 11

Conclusion

In this book on work-related learning and the social sciences, we have adopted two main approaches to the study of work. In the first part of the book, we constructed a series of theoretical frameworks with the aim of examining what can be gained from applying social scientific concepts to the way work is organised and its impact upon people. In the second part of the book, we have looked at what people can learn through work. It is now time to conclude our arguments and to draw connections between the various parts of the book and the various layers of the analysis.

Learning about work

In the first part of the book, we focused upon the ways in which work influences how individuals view their personal identities, power relations with colleagues, their place in the community and their responsibilities as citizens. We have made use of a number of concepts in the belief that these concepts will be familiar to students of the social sciences and should therefore be easily transferred to the study of work. Social scientists should be reasonably aware of such concepts as identity, alienation, power, conflict, resistance, social capital and community. The extent to which these concepts play an important part in the formal curriculum will no doubt differ, but they are key cornerstones of a social scientific understanding of the world. Social scientists might attempt to discern how individuals form their characters and develop their value systems. Family, education, peer groups, the media and work will all have an influence upon the way people see themselves. Social scientists might look at the power of the state and compare this with the power of other social institutions. They might think about the inequalities in power that stem from class, gender and ethnic divisions. It is our belief that studying work provides us with another way to understand how power relations operate on a local level. When looking to find an explanation for crime, drug use, unemployment and alienation, social scientists might investigate the role of the local community and consider why communities allow some members to drift and to become hostile. By looking at work in the community, we see how important it is for individuals to see themselves within a communal setting and to make appropriate contributions to the collective life of the community. We also attempt to investigate the responsibilities of citizens. Whilst in no way advocating that everybody should become politically active and socially engaged, we can see the benefits of people recognising their social and moral responsibilities and how these can be strengthened through work.

As work is a fundamental human activity that helps to define individuals, their place in society and the way they interact in the community, it should be of some interest to social scientists. To sociologists, studying work can reveal a great deal about social inequalities and the different roles people choose to take. Political scientists may well be more interested in the nature of conflict and resistance and in what work can reveal about power relations. Psychologists might be more inclined to pay attention to the way individuals view themselves, respond to peer pressure and group dynamics and the process by which they learn new skills. Case studies on working in the police force and examining the individual's role within the community might be of interest to criminologists. Social scientific approaches to work will differ significantly from approaches devised within a framework of business studies. Rather than ask how managers can secure the best possible return from their investments in human labour, social scientists will place work within a broader sociopolitical context. For social scientists, work is seen as part of the fabric of an individual's identity and a key influence in social systems.

In learning about work within this social and political context, we have shown an interest in how individuals create themselves and express their values. Whilst instabilities in the economic system and the increasing demands of employers might exert pressure upon workers, the search for fulfilment and creativity at work remains for many people. We affirm the importance of taking note of emotions and how these can be liberating or a source of frustration. Apart from anything else, it is important to find ways to overcome the fears stemming from work. Fear is not confined to those who are unable to find their feet at work or settle in a job or career. It is something that hits many people in different ways and should be taken into account when thinking about how to find suitable work.

Learning through work

The second part of the book dealt with *learning through work*. We have taken apart a number of key skills and have attempted to show how these skills can be developed. This material has been delivered within a framework of experiential learning and in the belief that individuals can advance by reflecting upon their experiences. Reflection helps people to gain an insight into the ways in which they reach conclusions about their work and their experiences. People might choose to reflect on their own or collectively. Reflection allows for experiences to be processed through taking the raw material of an incident or problem, making observations about it, drawing connections with conceptual frameworks and making plans for the future. In this way, individuals are able to view their experiences from a variety of angles and consider the implications of these experiences. By processing experiences in this way, and by taking account of the emotions generated, individuals can improve their understanding of work. In so doing, they can identify ways to rebalance their activities and make changes to the way they live and work. Reflection is a powerful tool, which can be used to understand experiences and give coherence to plans.

In looking for ways to develop work-related skills, we have attempted to reveal the processes involved in problem solving, decision making, creativity, leadership, teamwork and communication. We have pointed out, however, that these skills are rarely cultivated in isolation and that it is important to take into account how these skills relate to one another. Although it is possible to attend a course to improve communication skills, for example, the value of such a course will be enhanced through recognising the connection between communication skills, leadership, teamwork and problem solving. The selection of skills we have identified will seep into one another and together they represent a starting point for those who wish to consider how to develop not only individual skills but also their broader ability to work effectively. We have argued that individuals should see developing these skills as part of a long-term process to enhance their employability. This employability rests not only on the accumulation of skills but upon recognising the connection between the skills and perhaps their importance for particular roles or sectors of employment. Viewed in this way, developing employability can be seen as a part of ongoing personal development in much the same way as learning a new language, establishing a sensible programme for physical fitness or attempting to secure and maintain a healthy work-life balance.

The layers of analysis

Having identified the key stages in the narrative structure of this book, it is now time to revisit the layers used in the construction of arguments. We have looked for ways to learn from key social theorists, from the experiences of people who work in different sectors of employment and from the experiences of our students. Taken together, they provide us with a diverse portrait of the impact and potential of work.

The book has contained an overtly theoretical dimension. Part one of the book made extensive use of theoretical frameworks and drew upon the work of Marx, Foucault, Putnam, Bauman and Beck. These theorists are concerned not only with work but also with numerous economic, social, cultural and political issues. By making use of these theorists, we can see how work features in the construction of social and political theory. In part two of the book, we have drawn upon a range of educational theorists including Kolb, Belbin, Moon and Beard, Hochschild, Lave and Wenger and Fuller and Unwin who investigate the ways to translate experiences at work into meaningful narratives about individual and social life. These theorists help us to understand the importance of experiential learning and how this can be used as a framework for the development of skills and employability.

The second layer of analysis draws upon the experiences of workers from key sectors of employment. Examples have been given from low-skilled work and from some of the professions. The experiences of workers in low-skilled occupations are important in showing the impact of work on identity and on how workers adapt and respond to inequalities in power. We have also paid special attention to those areas popular with graduates of the social sciences by drawing upon the experience of workers in such areas as teaching, social work, the police, healthcare, journalism and the third sector. When looking at these key professions, we have attempted to show how workers develop their skills and understanding of their chosen sector and become more aware of their connections with others. We have seen that these careers are challenging. Although they involve attempting to help and empower other people, these careers can also be stressful because of high caseloads, challenging clients, antisocial behaviour, increasing levels of bureaucracy and the seemingly endless struggle for resources. We have also noted how workers in these sectors of employment will often need to find ways to develop their links with the community and frequently need to come to terms with their own responsibilities as citizens. Workers in these professions are expected to understand their roles in the community and to develop an appropriate social awareness and professional ethos.

Our students have provided us with the material for an additional layer of the analysis. Students often have to take on part-time jobs whilst they study. Whilst these jobs are necessary to help finance their studies, they can also create tensions for the students. In addition to the problems of balancing their jobs and their academic work, students can often find that they live in two very different worlds. On the one hand, they might be working in low-skilled and low-paid work where they need to find ways to motivate themselves, deal with mundane tasks and often feel isolated from full-time and permanent staff. On the other hand, they are studying for their degrees and starting to think about what they would like to do after graduation. The distance between these two worlds can increase as they progress through their degrees. Students have talked about feeling embarrassed, disempowered, squashed and disrespected in their jobs and how this differs greatly from their experience of studying for their degrees and the relationships they form with others at university. But the students also note that they need to learn how to make the best of their experiences as they prepare for graduation and for the challenge of new careers. Because of this, they will often come to realise the importance of work-related learning. This applies, in particular, when they are able to draw connections with their own academic discipline.

Conclusion

In this book, we have attempted to locate the individual within a work setting. We have been keen to show how work can touch people in many ways and how people can take an interest in the work they do and make choices that are appropriate for themselves. We have introduced some careers that students might consider and drawn attention to some of the skills needed to work in graduate-level occupations. We have seen that work-related learning provides another way to view individual and social life. This should not be seen as an alternative to academic learning, but as an important branch of education in the social sciences. It provides a way to link the theoretical material covered in lectures and seminars with experiences of living and working alongside one another. Developing an awareness of work and employability might help students see their experiences of work in a slightly different way, make plans for their future and consider how these plans relate to their own personal development.

Index